POLARIZATI

HEALTHIER CHURCH

Also by Ronald W. Richardson

*Family Ties That Bind: A Self-Help Guide to Change
through Family of Origin Therapy*

*Couples in Conflict: A Family Systems Approach
to Marriage Counseling*

Becoming Your Best: A Self-Help Guide for Thinking People

*Becoming a Healthier Pastor: Family Systems Theory
and the Pastor's Own Family*

*Creating a Healthier Church: Family Systems Theory,
Leadership, and Congregational Life*

With Lois Richardson

*Birth Order and You: How Your Sex and Position in
the Family Affects Your Personality and Relationships*

Polarization and the Healthier Church

Applying Bowen Family Systems Theory to Conflict and Change in Society and Congregational Life

Ronald W. Richardson

Polarization and the Healthier Church
Applying Bowen Family Systems Theory to Conflict and Change
in Society and Congregational Life
Ronald W. Richardson

ISBN-13: 978-1475006094

ISBN-10: 1475006098

About the Cover

The image on the cover is an artistic rendition of a photograph depicting a stained glass window. The variety of colors in the windows of churches worldwide often celebrate the beauty of God's love for all people in our diverse communities and cultures.

This photo, shown on the back cover in its original form, was distorted by pulling it at opposite ends so that it is no longer an accurate representation of the true window. The opposing forces that stretched and strained this image symbolize the effects of conflict and tension in our congregations, as well as in society.

This is the effect of polarization.

Photo by Ronald W. Richardson

Artistic Rendering by Lois A. Richardson

Book and Cover Design by Sharon K. Miller

For all the law is fulfilled in one word, even in this; Thou shalt love thy neighbour as thyself. But if ye bite and devour one another, take heed that ye be not consumed one of another.

—*Galatians* 5:14-15,
King James Version (KJV)

Because for some reason the human brain is open to polarities—to opposing viewpoints. And the human struggle wants to argue these viewpoints, and the media debates want to set up the polarities and get people to argue on them. So the human being is set up for arguing polarities. There is a never ending supply of polarities.

—Dr. Murray Bowen,
Bringing Systems Theory to Life

Contents

Preface 1

1—Positive Change in a Racially Polarized Situation 15

2—Understanding the Race Riot from a Family Systems
   Theory Perspective 27

3—The Triangle and Polarization in Family, Church, and
   Society 49

4—Differentiation of Self and Polarization 65

5—Emotional Process in Society and Polarization 83

6—Avoiding a Potentially Polarizing Situation in a Local
   Church 99

7—Avoiding Polarization in a Counseling Staff During
   Change 115

8—A Polarized Denominational Issue Handled Well 125

9—Concluding Thoughts on Leadership in Polarized
   Situations 135

Selected Bibliography 155

Bowen Family Systems Theory Training Opportunities 157

More Information on Dr. Murray Bowen and His Work 161

Preface

On one particular day, I am consulting with a pastor whose denomination, as well as her own congregation, is in the midst of a debate about both the ordination of gays and legalizing gay marriage. She does not know what to do with regard to her public stance in the church. She knows what she believes personally; she is in favor of both, but she does not know how to approach this topic with her congregation. When the time comes for her denominational vote, the congregation will know her position. She wants to know what she should do, given that influential members of her congregation openly oppose the positions she holds.

Then, later in the same day, I am consulting with a lay leader embroiled in heavy debate in his parish around the ongoing abortion battle. He is so angry about this that a friend suggested he seek counseling. He is against abortion for any reason. Even though he does not intend to be mean-spirited, he understands the feelings of those who have shot abortion doctors. He knows it is wrong and does not condone it, but he is "so torn up" that he does not know how to handle his anger at pro-choice advocates. He is especially angry with his pastor and certain members of his congregation who do not agree with him. They have had loud and unpleasant arguments. He asks me what I think. Is he unchristian in his attitude toward the pro-choice people, or is he "defending the faith?"

We live in polarizing times both in our churches and in our society. We are easily drawn into emotionally intense arguments with others who take positions that are opposite of our views.

Examples of polarization exist within every human community: in our families, in our neighborhoods, between friends, in our arts and cultural life, in our workplaces, and, of course, in the church. Conflict is all too common in our various communities. This book offers a way to understand the polarizing process and what each of us can do to reduce its intensity and to promote positive change. Each one of us, whether an elected or appointed leader, or a church member, can do something to reduce polarization and contribute to a healthier community.

This is not a book on how to improve communication, as important as that is. There are numerous other resources for dealing with differences through better communication. However, when there is a high degree of emotional intensity, efforts to communicate often make things more combative. Dialogues quickly degenerate into angry confrontations. Meaningful communication, though, is a result of a larger process. When people understand and engage in that process, communication improves, and most likely, they will realize they do not need a course on how to do it.

In order to engage in this process, we need a larger understanding of how human beings function in society and in our relationships with one another, especially in an atmosphere of emotional intensity. That is what I intend to bring to readers of this book. If we stay narrowly focused on the issues themselves (by either arguing them or trying to mediate them), we will stay stuck in our efforts to deal with them. By enlarging the picture of what is involved when these heated debates arise, we can discover new avenues for approaching them. We can get on with living the gospel message with one another and being the church ministering in a world of turmoil and division.

What is polarization?

My dictionary gives three definitions for "polarization:" The first one explains the scientific concept, that is, "the deposition of gas on one or both electrodes of an electrolytic cell increasing the resistance and setting up a counter electromotive force." The application of a catalyst, such as the gas in this definition, can apply to a lot of polarizing talk, but the most relevant aspect in this definition is the issue of electrical resistance and counter force. When someone takes one strongly polarized stance, say in a church meeting, others often say they can "feel the electricity in the air;" that is, things get "charged" because they know someone else in the meeting will react and take the opposite position.

Another definition comes from the field of magnetics and speaks of "the division of a field into two opposites." We think of magnetic forces repelling each other, but what this also implies is that the opposing forces are part of the same field; they have a lot in common. In polarized circumstances, we ignore or forget this fact.

Focusing on the cultural phenomenon of polarization brings us to the third definition, which is "the concentration of opposing extremes of groups or interests formally ranged on a continuum." It is normal for human communities to hold a range of opinions along a continuum on nearly any topic. Normally, people in groups do not all think the same. Life would be dull if that were the case. In polarization, as an electrified atmosphere of opposing forces, people begin to regard those who do not think like they do as the enemy. As the intensity of feelings increases, they seek to defeat and even humiliate or destroy one another. Respect for others is lost. The ethic of love gives way to the ethic of hate. I have heard good Christians speak of how much they hate the people on the other side of an issue.

Civil discussion of important issues, in recent years, has become more difficult to achieve. Those on each side believe they are morally right, as well as politically superior, and they see the other side in more negative, if not in morally evil, terms. In these circumstances, calm and reasoned group discussion of an issue is less likely. Each side makes negative assertions about the other side, questions their motives, and uses inflammatory images to characterize the other's position.

Most Christians know the parable of the Good Samaritan (Luke 10:25-37, KJV). A lawyer, who was an expert in Jewish religious law, asked Jesus, "What must I do to inherit eternal life?" Instead of answering his question, Jesus asked him what the law prescribes, and the man replied, "Thou shalt love the Lord thy God with all thy heart, and with all thy soul, and with all thy strength, and with all thy mind; and thy neighbour as thyself." Jesus assented, saying, "Correct. Do this and you will live." But the lawyer, hoping to trick Jesus, asked another question much debated in those days. Referring to the second commandment to love our neighbor, the man asked, "And who is my neighbor?" He wanted Jesus to tell him who was within the circle of being a neighbor, who was outside the circle, whom he should love, and whom he could ignore or even condemn. He was an expert at drawing lines between those people who were acceptable and those who were not.

It was then, in his response, that Jesus told the story about a Jewish man who was travelling from Jerusalem to Jericho. He was set upon by thieves, stripped naked, beaten, robbed, and left for dead by the side of the road. First, a priest saw the man and passed by, ignoring him, and then a Levite did the same. Both of these men were experts in the law and the commandments. They were good people. But it was a Samaritan who came upon him, took pity on him, attended to his wounds, and clothed him. Afterwards, he took him to an inn and paid the innkeeper to give him whatever he needed for healing.

The Jews and the Samaritans hated each other. The Samaritans were thought to be the remnant of the lost northern tribe of Israel, but their beliefs were significantly different from the orthodox Jews of the day. They were considered unclean, irreligious, and heretical. They were "too different" to be considered neighbors by most Jews. The historian Josephus tells us there were many clashes and battles between the two groups during the time of Jesus.

As he finished the story, Jesus asked the lawyer, "Who was a neighbor to the robbed and beaten man?" The lawyer could only answer, "The one who showed mercy on him." Because of the enmity between them, he could not even bring himself to say, "The Samaritan."

Notice how Jesus changed the lawyer's question from "Who is my neighbor?" to "Who behaved like a neighbor?" He challenged him, and, thereby, he challenges us to behave like caring neighbors toward those who are different from us, not just those we know to be on our side. In doing so, as Jesus said, we fulfill all of the law and the prophets. The apostle Paul apparently knew this story because he referred to the same standard in his letter to the Galatians, which is quoted in one of this book's epigraphs. If we "bite and devour one another" we will be consumed by these hostilities (*Galatians* 5:14-15).

This book is, in essence, about how to define ourselves as neighbors to those with whom we disagree in fundamental ways. Just as the enmity between the Samaritans and the Jews was a critically important issue in Jesus' day, so are there many contentious issues in contemporary society; thus, his is a relevant question for us today. Are we behaving like neighbors toward those with whom we disagree?

I will not give you easy answers to this question. Jesus did not tell the lawyer what it would take to have the personal character to behave like the Samaritan. However, readers of this book will learn an approach to dealing with the polarizing contemporary issues that will help clarify a path for ourselves. I offer personal examples of what has worked in my ministry as a pastor, a counselor, and a consultant in a variety of settings.

I do not offer ways to put an end to differences between people on important issues. This is both impossible and undesirable.

Neither Jesus nor Paul ignored the issues over which people disagreed, but the problem—then and now—is not in our differences. We can relate to one another in positive ways while also addressing these important issues.

In much of the Middle East, as in Iraq, for example, the religious divisions of Sunni, Shiite, and Kurdish tribes contribute to an ongoing conflict that will not soon be resolved. In tribal societies, loyalty to the tribe is more important than to any larger entity like "a nation." This is true of polarized groups in western society. In the United States and Canada, our own political (tribal) warfare is a powerful threat to democracy. One side accuses the other of partisanship while engaging in the practice itself. As a result, our problems as a society remain unresolved while generating even more heat.

We have all witnessed it, and perhaps we have even participated in it. I certainly have been a participant. As a liberal pastor back in the 1960s, and as part of a liberal takeover of the social mission of the Presbyterian Church in those early days, I certainly did my part to help fan the flames of division, even though that was not my intent. I thought I was doing something good.

The church is not just a victim of this process. In some cases, it has been an instigator of it. The divisions between members of a congregation and between congregations within a denomination have grown to overwhelming proportions. Some churches have intentionally generated and heightened the polarization process, from both the liberal and conservative sides. If you are happy with the present state of things in our society and in our churches, then this book is not for you.

Polarization is also a family issue. When I was a young man, my mother outlawed all discussion of politics and religion when I came home for visits because my atheist stepfather and I had frequent, heated arguments around both topics. My mother had married him after I left home; consequently, he and I did not have a relationship history. He was a Los Angeles police officer based in the Ramparts district, which included Watts. (He was there when the Watts riots broke out in 1965.) I was an inner-city pastor working in an African American neighborhood of a northeastern city in the United States. He and I were as strongly polarized as the society we were each a part of. I kept trying to get him to see his racism and its impact on his police work, and he kept challenging what he thought were my naïve political and social beliefs that either excused or gave license to criminals and bad guys. Neither one of us was able to persuade the other to change his mind. We did little to explore each other's own thinking.

A different approach

There is no good research on how to overcome polarization, but starting in the 1970s, I began to use a different approach to these sociopolitical issues with some degree of success. This book is about what I began to learn then and have been able to refine since that time. Even though what I offer here is based on personal experience, I believe that through thoughtful analysis of how people function in social relationships, we can make a good start by challenging polarization and working to create a civil society. He is long dead, but if I had the chance to relive the relationship with my stepfather, I would take a very different stance.

The approach I use suggests clear ways to mitigate the polarizing process and bring about positive change over time. I base this on an understanding of human behavior called Bowen family systems theory. I will offer a number of personal experiences, both as a pastor and as a clinician, which can lead to a healthier congregational life in the midst of a polarized community, as well as to more effective mission action in this divided world. Anyone can do what I describe in this book. It does not require a professional role to do it, although some personal growth may be required. It was for me.

In this book, I offer an option that I think of as "the way of wisdom." I spoke of this in an earlier book, *Creating a Healthier Church* (1996). Jesus is the exemplar of wisdom. Ethically, Jesus defined himself as a neighbor to all kinds of people who were considered unacceptable in mainstream religious communities. The only people he really condemned were those who defined themselves as better, or more correct, than others. Like the lawyer who confronted Jesus, the Pharisees were experts at dividing good from bad, right from wrong, and separating themselves from anything unclean. They were the great polarizers of that time.

In my earliest days of ministry (in the 1960s), I thought of my pastoral role in mostly prophetic terms. I wanted to persuade people of the "wrongness" of their social beliefs, and I tried to convince them, in my preaching and teaching, to think about things the way I did. This intent, to get others to think the way we do, is a key ingredient in the polarizing process. I did not understand this at the time.

This book is also a memo to myself, to remind me to keep doing what I, in fact, know how to do. I know personally that our passions can overtake us. I can be extremely passionate on any number of topics. Our strong commitment to certain principles as a society can get in the way of living out other principles related to the importance of community. In part, reducing the amount of polarization in our communities is a values clarification process. This book raises the question of what is ultimately important to us. The extended personal example in the first chapter shows how I struggled with that question and achieved success in a highly polarized situation.

The church did not invent this polarizing process. It is endemic to human community and is as old as Adam and Eve. Another epigraph for this book—this one from Dr. Bowen—affirms this. He points out that the "human brain is open to polarities—to opposing viewpoints." Moreover, as a normal human process, the intensity of polarization waxes and wanes with the rising and falling of social anxiety throughout history. At this time, it is obviously rising significantly.

This is not a book on conflict resolution. Most of those kinds of approaches involve an expert practitioner doing something to, with, or for others, along with instituting certain procedures that others must follow in order to initiate change. I will not offer a recipe of sorts, such as, "five easy steps to overcome polarization." Instead, I offer an approach that does not require the cooperation of others to get change to happen. It is not about what we can do to or for others. It is about change in self, based on an understanding of how we, as human beings, tend to function in high anxiety situations, and it is about how to *be* with others differently. To the extent that we are successful in our own efforts, there is greater likelihood that positive change will occur in the larger community.

The way of wisdom does not mean that everyone must think and feel the same way. We can believe in a unity of disparate parts. Even though it is a cliché, it is still true that it takes all parts of the rainbow to create its beauty. As *Genesis* (9:13-16, KJV), reminds us, the varied color of the rainbow is a sign of hope. Paul's organic image of the body (*1 Corinthians* 12:12-31, KJV) continues to be a useful metaphor for the church. We are not all the same. We not only look different from one another, there are differences in how we think, believe, and feel, as well as how we function and act. Unity is not equivalent to sameness. To be part of an organic whole does not require sameness. It simply requires an affirmation of the importance of each part of the body.

Bowen family systems theory

Many readers of this book are already familiar with Bowen theory. For other readers, Bowen systems theory may be a new approach to understanding how the human community works. This book is an extension of my two previous books on the church and leadership: *Creating a Healthier Church* (1996), and

Becoming a Healthier Pastor (2004). Those books are more exhaustive in defining the kind of organizational and personal work I only refer to in this book. In this book, I assume a certain degree of understanding of the theory by the reader. I must refer readers, for space reasons, to other works (see the bibliography) for a fuller presentation of Bowen family systems theory and its application to communities like the church. As this text progresses, I provide brief explanations of the relevant aspects of the theory rather than a full systematic presentation of the Bowen family systems theory. Chapters two through five elaborate on some important aspects of the theory with reference to the theme of polarization.

Bowen theory is not the only wisdom for dealing with the difficulties of polarization. Some of the positive personal pastoral experiences I offer here occurred long before I ever heard of Murray Bowen and his theory of human functioning. However, his theory could have predicted the positive outcome of my pastoral functioning back then. This fact demonstrates that he did not invent or create the mechanisms that lead to a healthier human community; he simply identified and gave names to these long-standing ways of human functioning. He referred to the principles I describe as a "distant drumbeat" that has been present in humans from the beginning of life. He brought an understanding of these mechanisms together into a coherent theory that heightens our ability to understand the emotional processes of human life and to function more effectively in the church and society.

Bowen theory strives to be scientific and descriptive, not normative. It describes, as best it can, what *is*, rather than what *should be*. It simply explains how we function and the dynamics that are involved. A Bowen purist would not speak of people or institutions as healthy or not. They are what they are. The word "health" implies some relationship to sickness or to the absence of sickness. To them, it is not helpful to speak of "sick" churches. As people of faith, however, we are interested in ethical and normative issues as well as theological ones. We assert some values over others.

Therefore, because I bring my faith position to Bowen theory, I do use the word "healthy," which Dr. Bowen would not do. While his position makes sense to me, I use the term to mean the ability to maintain a sense of balance or equilibrium even in the face of stress and adversity. This fits with the biological concept of a healthy body. When a church is healthy, it is functioning at an optimum level so that its congregational life promotes its purpose for existing.

Who this book is for and how it is organized

Church members, whether they are pastors or lay people, who are concerned about issues that divide their congregations will find this book useful. By exploring the problems it describes and learning about the process of building a healthier community life, we will restore the sense of balance and equilibrium our church community needs. We do not have to be elected officers or appointed leaders to either hinder or help this process. Leadership does not reside so much in holding an official position as it does in our way of being a member of a group.

My focus here is the church, but because the church is only one part of the larger society, I hope this book will also have an effect on society. The larger culture influences us in the church and we can impact that culture. Throughout history, the church has nurtured many great social and political leaders; thus, the values of the church have influenced society for centuries. We still do so today.

None of the successes I describe in this book could have happened without the healthy functioning of other people. They were able to overcome the polarizing forces at work within themselves. I regard them as the true heroes of my stories. However, I did have something to do with their successes. I take credit for my part in achieving these successes and, through utilizing Bowen theory, explain why my actions and those of others worked effectively to bring about change.

In the first chapter, I provide an extended example of an act of social ministry in a racially polarized situation that occurred in the community where I was a pastor in 1971. Because I had departed from my prophetic stance of the 1960s, my work led to a significantly different outcome than I might have achieved otherwise. This chapter describes one dramatic example of how that ministry worked.

In the second chapter, I analyze the event in the first chapter using Bowen family systems theory. Even though the theory was unknown to me at the time, I understand, in retrospect, my unconscious sense of how to handle this situation reflects much of Bowen theory. It is why I was successful in my approach to the problem.

In the next chapters, I explore important concepts in the theory and elaborate on the aspects of personal functioning that can challenge the dynamics of polarization.

In later chapters, I provide additional examples of my successful ministry in polarized circumstances. These stories demonstrate how the theory works in action. In my training programs for other church leaders, I have seen how this approach has worked well for them also.

In the final chapter, I summarize the important attributes needed for effective pastoral and lay leadership in polarized situations. Much of this, I learned through my own experience and learned later, in my study of Bowen family systems theory, why it was so effective.

Acknowledgements

I want to thank my good friends, Doug Anderson and Randy Frost, for reading the manuscript for this book. Their friendship over many years has been invaluable to me. They know my limitations as a writer and as an interpreter of Bowen family systems theory for the general public, and yet they continue to read my efforts and comment on them for my edification and improvement of the text. Their dear friendship, and yet their willingness to be my critics, has been a boon to me and to you, the readers.

This book focuses on the eighth concept in Bowen theory, which is the emotional process in society. Pat Comella has concentrated on this concept and has read much of the manuscript for this book. Pat is a busy lawyer, an international mediator, and a member of the faculty of the Georgetown Family Center in Washington, DC. I have learned from her work, and some of her thinking informs chapter five. None of my readers would put the theory quite the way I do, and yet they have been tolerant and appreciative of my unique approach.

A final thank you goes to my editor, Sharon Miller, for her struggles with my failure to express myself adequately in the English language. Editors are the unsung heroes of books that have been perfected through their work. My wife Lois, who is also an editor, and who wisely refuses to touch my work, has a t-shirt that says, "To write is human, to edit is divine." I have learned to agree with her.

1

Positive Change in a Racially Polarized Situation

The background

The outer-city Presbyterian church where I served as pastor was in a middle-sized city in the northeastern United States. Although the church was once a vital part of the neighborhood, things had changed significantly by the time I arrived in February of 1970. Its membership was just under 300 people as many former members had moved to the suburbs. The immediate community was changing from a mixed blue- and white-collar, all Caucasian, primarily Roman Catholic population to a much poorer, black population. The church was not attracting new members from this different population, and church leaders knew they had to do a better job of relating to changes in the surrounding neighborhood—the neighborhood they sought to serve.

The church members who remained were mostly older, retired people with good intentions, but they had never related closely to people of a different race. It was clear, at the time, that they were not personally equipped to develop the changed attitudes they needed to welcome the new neighborhood people. For example, early in my first year, as a result of some cold calling I did in the neighborhood, a black man came to our Sunday worship service. One of the first people I introduced him to, a leader in the church, demonstrated the problem. I said, "Harriet, I would like to introduce you to Mr. Joe Johnson." Before I could say anything else, she said, "Oh, is this our new janitor?" He never returned. Harriet had a good heart, but her long-held attitudes had not prepared her for the changes everyone in the church said they wanted.

My call to this church included a ministry within the community. Part of the reason they called me was that I had served for four years as an associate pastor in an integrated, inner-city church in another eastern city. In addition to regular pastoral duties there, I had been the director of a church-sponsored community center that provided a broad range of social, educational, and recreational services to the poor, black community in which it was located.

I accepted the call to the new church because I wanted to minister to the people this church now had the opportunity to serve: a community of blue- and white-collar Caucasians. Rather than focus on the needs of the poor, black community, which by then had many advocates (and the necessary black leadership), I wanted to minister to the white people in this church and to those with unrecognized and unmet needs who still lived in its community. As part of what was then called "the silent majority," they saw themselves as taken for granted and underserved. One Presbytery colleague characterized my efforts as "a ministry to Archie Bunker." I did not quite see it that way but understood his meaning. His was an attitude typical of the more liberal members of my Presbytery.

The event

Early in my second year at the church, my secretary rushed into my office to say, "Ron, there is a race riot going on at the high school. I just got a call that the police are there." Without really thinking about what I was going to do, I put on my clergy shirt and collar (to legitimize my presence) and dashed over to the school. An eight-foot high chain-link fence surrounded the school property. On the city-block-size playground inside the fence, there were many hundreds of angry students. Clearly, from the blood that I saw on peoples' faces and clothing, there had just been some vicious fighting. When I arrived, the police (thirty or forty of them) had separated the students into two groups—one black and one white. Even so, students were still angrily taunting and challenging each other with name-calling and racial epithets.

Looking at the group of black students, I saw about ten white adults whom I took to be teachers. They were trying to calm the black students. There were also several black pastors among them, recognizable by their clergy collars. It was clear to me that there was plenty of adult leadership available. When I looked at the white students, there were no adults (not even teachers) among them except for the police. The police were barely able to hold them back. I was the only white pastor present.

On the street side of the chain-link fence were approximately thirty white adults. They were mostly parents, shouting at their children; their intent was not to calm them down but to rile them up further. They were just as angry as their children were. They were egging them on, shouting vicious, racial epithets, and telling them not to take any more from "the niggers." This polarized situation had been brewing for a long time and now it was boiling over. I said to myself, "Okay Ron, these are the people you said you wanted to minister to." I swallowed hard and knew that I was going to wade into a swamp full of unexplored danger.

My approach

I approached the white parents and asked them what was going on. Their response was an angry wave of racial invective aimed both at the school and at the black community. Saul Alinsky, a nationally known community organizer, had helped to organize the black community in this city. Actually, he was someone I admired. His black community group had become a powerful force in the city. White people felt like they were the target of much of the black anger, and with the increasing political power of black people, white people thought they were losing out in many ways, including in the education of their children.

I invited these parents to meet at my church that evening to talk in greater depth about their complaints. Much to my surprise, nearly fifty parents gathered in the church basement that evening, venting through angry, race-based attacks and complaints about the poor treatment their kids were getting from the school district. I served as moderator, and as I tried to guide the "conversation" toward some more specific statement of the issues, I felt like I was at the head of a lynch mob.

With no particular direction emerging, we concluded the evening with my suggestion that we return in a week's time, which would give me time to think about what I was doing. I asked the parents to invite others who would be interested, and then we could decide on a plan of action. The next day I called members of my church board and told them what I had done. I had their support, and two of them said they would come to the next meeting.

The next week over 300 angry, white parents showed up for the meeting. I was amazed. They were mostly members of two local Roman Catholic parishes, and they had told people at their churches about the meeting. From the start, and throughout this whole process, I tried to involve the priests at these churches, but they were "not available." This group of parents proved to be just as angry as the ones from the previous week, and, like the others, their language was laced with profanity and racial invective. No one challenged them or suggested that they should "cool it" with the racist language, including me. I continued to wear my collar, and because they were Catholics, group members automatically referred to me as "Father." I decided I would not make a point of correcting them or focusing on their crude language and racist attitudes. Instead, I chose to avoid communicating any sign of moral condemnation.

Still, what I was doing at the head of this mob was not clear to me. I had a high level of anxiety that I think I managed to keep hidden. I had, in prior years, worked with large groups of angry black people talking this way about "whitey." Curiously, even as a white person, I had been more comfortable with them than here with these angry white people.

I tried to keep a positive focus during the evening's "discussion" and had a large pad of newsprint on which I wrote their complaints. At the end of that evening, I tried to summarize what I called "valid" complaints that we should try to resolve. I suggested we form a parents' action group and elect officers at the next meeting, form a steering committee, and develop some ideas for how we might proceed. Everyone agreed. The two church board members in attendance were supportive of the effort, but the venomous language they had heard that evening unnerved them, and they decided they would not come back. I was disappointed but told them I understood. Even though no members of the board attended additional meetings, they continued to support my efforts.

How the work evolved

At the next meeting, a similar number of people showed up. I had privately spoken with a few people in the group whom I thought had the most positive stances and encouraged them to run for office. As it turned out, they were among those nominated by the larger group, and we came out of the next meeting with some good people to serve as a steering committee. I worked with this group to establish an agenda for the next meeting. We called ourselves the Northeast White Parents' Association.

In the meetings that followed, we decided to focus on the city's school board and the superintendent of schools. We learned that at this particular high school, ten white teachers had been assigned reduced teaching schedules so they could work with the black students, helping them deal with the racial attitudes they encountered and develop better study habits. They provided extra counseling help, along with a range of other services. None of these services were available to the white students. Furthermore, these teachers taught a required course in "sensitivity training" to the white students, which focused primarily on their racism. The course only served to inflame the already hostile feelings among the white students and their parents.

I discovered that there was a white teacher, Hal, who was admired by both parents and students. I got to know Hal and learned that he was a tough, no-nonsense, old-style Roosevelt Democrat with whom I could easily share some of my thinking about this effort. He agreed to work full time with this group of white students and to help me with the parents if the school board and the principal approved. I was happy at the prospect of having someone who could share the load with me. I needed to get back to my regular pastoral duties and I had confidence in Hal.

The steering committee members came to the next school board meeting with me, and we asked for time on the agenda. I had called the superintendent earlier and told him to expect us, and he showed some sympathy for my concerns. Happily, the board agreed to release Hal immediately from his teaching duties and to pay him to work full time with our white student and parent groups. They could hardly refuse this request because of the ten teachers who were already working with the black students. However, the board proved to be uninterested in the rest of our concerns about the educational needs of the students. They said they would wait and see how things developed with Hal.

By now, our group was becoming well known. The little that the local media reported on us focused negatively on the white students, our parents' group, and our efforts. At the same time, my uneasiness with what I was doing diminished somewhat, now that I thought things were heading in a positive direction. However, I received no support from the denominational staff or my clergy friends and colleagues. None of my liberal friends, even at the local community organization, thought I should be doing what I was doing. They all said that I was organizing a racist, "White Power" organization. Even Lois, my wife, thought I was in dangerous territory and warned me against continuing. I understood their doubts about the wisdom of my actions; I frequently had similar doubts.

The only people who understood what I was doing were the black pastors I knew. They were part of the Alinsky "Black Power" group that had already had a big impact in the city. In fact, their nationally recognized organization had often been in the news as they clashed with large corporations based in this city. They had successfully demonstrated that the corporations had engaged in discriminatory hiring and promotion. They said, "Ron, we think it's great what you are doing. We have been so frustrated that we have had no one in that group of people to deal with."

In spite of wearing my white collar at our meetings, my clergy status never deterred anyone, as far as I could tell, from saying exactly what they wanted to say in the way they wanted to say it. In the course of our discussions, occasionally someone would say, "Excuse me, Father, but this is what I've got to say . . ." and then launch into some profanity-filled, racist invective.

One of the early high points for me came during this initial phase of the work. One evening, after a heated meeting with the larger group, I was standing outside of my church with the president of the group talking about the meeting. During this conversation, the president interrupted himself, looked at me intently, and said, "Father, why are you doing this? The churches have treated us like shit." This comment hit me in a powerful way. It said to me that I was getting through to them and that I was demonstrating something of what the gospel meant in this concrete situation. In response, I managed to say something like "important things are coming out in all of this" and that I thought, "attention should be paid."

Hal, the teacher, proved to be a real gift to the effort and he worked hard at it. He was an active member of a Baptist church in the suburbs but complained that he could not interest his pastor in what we were doing. He also discovered a man by the name of Jerry, who was a trained and credentialed mediator at the international level. Jerry met with Hal and me, and he quickly became interested in what we were doing and said to let him know if he could ever be of help.

Some time later, in talking with the black pastors, I discovered that they had some of the same complaints about education at this school that the white parents had. I wondered aloud with them what it would be like to have some of the black parents and white parents sit down together one evening and to talk about their concerns. We would make the discussion of racial issues off-limits, but instead focus on the concerns of the parents for their children's future. The black pastors bought in enthusiastically. Hal also thought this was a good idea and we decided to organize it.

There was no hesitation on the part of the white parents, which surprised me. The meeting between black and white parents went very well (after some natural, initial discomfort and hesitation). No one talked about race. Instead, both black and white parents, in response to my questions, expressed concern about their children's education. They discovered they had common concerns and could support a common agenda. At the end of the meeting, both groups said that they wanted to continue having these kinds of meetings. They took their excitement back to their respective groups and reported on the meeting. Even though Hal and I had been apprehensive about the meeting, we were surprised and gratified. The black pastors agreed to work with us to set up a number of these meetings, which occurred over a period of several months. I asked Jerry to work with Hal on setting up and running these meetings and they did an excellent job, keeping the focus on what we wanted from the school board. That "we" were now an integrated group of parents with a common mission had seemed improbable just weeks before.

In total, there were about thirty such interracial parent meetings (involving approximately ten to twelve parents), and they all went well. Some groups met only once, but many continued meeting throughout the next year. Not unexpectedly, the white parents began to experience a shift in their attitudes toward the black parents, and probably vice versa, even though race had never been a focus of our meetings. Racial epithets and profanity disappeared and the level of anger from the white parents dissolved when they discussed common goals.

The successful outcome

I left more and more of the work in the hands of Hal and Jerry, and I was happy to have the time once again to focus on other important needs of my church community. I continued to meet with the steering committee, and I would show up occasionally in the larger group. The result of the mixed-race parent meetings was the development of a common agenda for the education of both black and white students. However, after several meetings with the school board and its various representatives, it was clear that the board was not prepared to take action to implement our agenda. The liberal, white teachers had lobbied against our white parents' group. They were angry at our "racism" and refused to see anything positive in the interracial partnership that we had forged.

In spite of this rejection—or maybe because of it—our united parents' groups were even more intent on pursuing their goals. Then, at one joint meeting with the leadership of the two groups, Jerry proposed that they run their own slate of officers for the school board. Jerry and I had discussed this before, but we wondered if the parents would go for it. They did—enthusiastically. They set out to create a mixed-race slate of well-qualified candidates who were in touch with the goals of each group. By now, various professional-level church members

23

had come forward in support of our work. After sitting in on our meetings with the parents, it was clear to them that the slate of candidates were good candidates for the school board. Of course, the groups had hundreds of volunteers who were ready to campaign for them.

Most of the original angry, white parents continued to participate in this new effort, although they were not so angry anymore. They were quite positive about what was happening. Again, we never directly spoke about race as an issue. The air of polarized anger had dissipated. They focused their efforts on electing these nine black and white school board members. Amazingly, all nine of them were elected and they constituted an entirely new school board.

I left that city in the summer of 1976, but I heard, later, from friends that this group of white and black parents continued to put up a slate for the school board at each election in subsequent years. Twenty years after that first election, they still comprised the whole board. With a more responsive school board, the parents were more satisfied with what the schools were offering their children. Overall, the process took nearly two years from the date of the school riot to the election of the first school board slate. My church realized only a couple of new members because of this activity, but, ultimately, that was not what it was all about. The church did, however, earn a great deal of respect in the neighborhood and in the city. It was good for the spirit of the congregation.

Conclusion

I believe that my early intervention and involvement with the white parents' group short-circuited the full development of the polarizing process. The element I brought to the process was an intense curiosity about what was going on and how people were dealing with what they perceived to be the problem. I only asked questions in the early stages of our meetings. I took their answers seriously and each answer became an occasion for more questions from me. My questions, because they were non-evaluative in nature and did not attack the integrity of the parents, helped them to think things through more carefully.

If a more partisan and dictatorial person had become involved, one who took advantage of the passions of the group to shape the direction for his or her own purposes, then surely a very different and much less favorable outcome would have resulted. The group would have gone in the direction all of my friends and colleagues feared it inevitably would.

This piece of social ministry, focused on a highly polarized situation involving violence between racial groups, occurred long before I knew anything about Bowen theory. I had no framework to help me understand it at the time. I had not yet even begun to think about getting training as a pastoral counselor. I had an interest in the parallels between personal and social change, and this experience heightened that interest. The change in the white parents made a kind of intuitive sense, but I lacked a theory for how and why it worked. Now I understand why it worked in terms of the Bowen family systems theory.

In the following chapters, I offer some generalizations about how leadership can best function in polarized situations.

2

Understanding the Race Riot from a Family Systems Theory Perspective

What is a system?

We can understand the race riot situation, and its larger context, from the perspective of family systems theory. In a system, the action of one part affects the behavior of all of the other parts connected to it. No single part is responsible for the action of the whole, but each part contributes to the whole and makes it what it is. All parts are interconnected. No single part can be isolated from the others and treated as a separate entity. The white parents and white students at this high school were part of a larger, community-wide system.

It is common to think that particular individuals or groups cause problems in a community. This kind of thinking is automatic. Clearly, these individuals and groups (like the white parents and their children) act in problematic ways. We tend not to see the interconnections between people and the mutual influence that takes place. Murray Bowen (1978) called this "observational blindness;" that is, we have difficulty evaluating our own observations of others and their influence on us in a systematic way. We "can fail to see what is in front of us unless it fits into our theoretical frame of reference" (105).

We belong to many different systems over our lifetime. The first powerful system we belong to is the family in which we grow up. This system deeply affects our development, and we have an impact on it. Because, physically and emotionally, we spend approximately the first twenty years of our life in that system—our formative years—we remain sensitive to the influence of this system for the rest of our lives. This early experience shapes who we are in ways we do not always understand even when we become adults. As we grow and venture out into the world, we enter school systems, friendship systems, community group systems, faith group systems, work systems, as well as many others, all of which shape us and, in a reciprocal way, we shape them.

The white parents' group existed within a broad web of relational systems not of their choosing. The federal and state legislatures passed laws, and the courts made decisions based on those laws that the parents and their children were required to obey. The school administration had academic policies and disciplinary procedures that affected their children. The police, the courts, and the school administration, at one level or another, enforced these measures.

Systems are composed of counterbalancing forces. When these forces are in or near equilibrium, people are more relaxed, but they become uneasy and anxious when the forces are out of balance. When, over time, the imbalance becomes severe, then symptoms erupt. This is true of systems at all levels from the family and beyond, including neighborhoods, cities, states, nations, and the ecological systems of the earth. The race riot at the school was a symptom of a social system imbalance. As a symptom, it was an effect of other processes at work in the social system. The race riot did not cause the imbalance.

The negative behavior of any one part of a system (for example, whites attacking blacks at a school) is understood within the larger perspective of these counterbalancing forces. A family of an adolescent with behavior problems has parallels here. Focusing only on the child's bad behavior, which is simply a symptom, is to miss the larger, dynamic process of interacting in reciprocal family processes.

Last year I broke a bone in my right wrist while hiking. It was a simple break and no surgery was required, but it took about seven weeks for the bone to mend. When the doctor pronounced me "healed," I said, "But my hand still has lots of pain, and there are still so many things I can't do." He said, "Ah, yes, but I am a bone doctor. I don't fix hands."

His focus was on just the one part that he knew was broken, the symptom. The X-rays showed him that. He ignored everything else. This simple break affected the soft tissue in my hand and lower arm. There was a significant amount of pain and limited use of my lower arm and hand. My wife, Lois, had to help me with everyday things like taking a shower and drying off. As it happened, we were moving into a new house around that time. I could not fully participate in the packing, cleaning, unpacking, and moving things from the old to the new house. That little bone break affected not only my body's ability to function effectively, it also affected my ability to function as part of a family. We called on friends and new neighbors for help with particular needs related to the move. They changed schedules in their own lives to help us. Thus, my problem affected other people—some that I had never even met. Many systematic ripples went out into the world from this simple little bone break.

The emotional system

Dr. Murray Bowen began to develop family systems theory in the late 1940s. He was a psychiatry professor at Georgetown University in Washington, D.C. His theory describes how people function in close, emotional relationships and consists of eight basic concepts. He quickly realized that his theory could be of use not only to families in trouble, but also, for example, to organizations like the church. Bowen theory is at the core of much of the healthy church movement.

Emotionality is a powerful force within human systems. The more emotionally locked-in we are to the system, the less we are able to control our part in the interactive process. For example, when shoved, many people want to shove back. Some do and some do not, but the impulse is there. We get emotional chain reactions throughout a system when any one member has difficulty controlling his or her own part. "Fusion" is the name for this emotionally locked-in quality. In other words, our behavior is "fused" to the behaviors of others in the system when our actions are reactions to their behaviors and their actions are reactions to our behaviors. Such a chain reaction is endless. This emotional reactivity defines much of the intense conflict in the race riot situation.

When we set out to fix only the one part of a system that seems to be broken, other parts that are equally involved may be neglected or unrecognized; consequently, things do not get better. A focus on the one part (like the "sensitivity training" of the young, white students) only intensifies the imbalance. On a much larger scale, when a government passes civil rights laws with the intent of fixing unfair aspects of a country's racial functioning, it inevitably affects other parts of the national emotional system.

This is part of what led to the school race riot. Most people did not make this connection and simply blamed the white kids (and their parents, of course) for not being able to adjust to change. In fact, the more the teachers focused on the "bad" white kids' racist attitudes, the worse the problems got. School officials, as the supposed problem solvers, did not see themselves as part of the problem.

Each of the members of the white parents' group came from a family context that had also shaped their lives in significant ways. They came from multigenerational families that helped to shape their thinking, beliefs, feelings, and assumptions about life (including racial attitudes, for example). From that context, some of them had grown up to be mature and responsible adults who felt less like victims of the society they lived in. They harbored fewer intense racist attitudes. Others were less mature and were much more reactive to the outside forces in their lives, which they perceived as threatening. They focused less on their own goals in life, accepted less responsibility for those goals, and focused more on getting back at those whom they thought were oppressing them—those whom they thought were "the problem." Happily, in selecting officers and a steering committee, the group gravitated to the more mature members of the group. These people were moderately less reactive and more discerning about what they perceived was a real threat to the future of their children, and what was not.

The togetherness and individuality forces

In all living systems, there are two universal life forces that require balance. These are the togetherness and the individuality forces. The togetherness force is part of the emotional life of people that impels them to be involved with each other. Without this force, we would have no social life. This desire to connect closely to other people is part of why we marry and create families, as well as joining other social groups, including our church. This force seeks to bind us together in various configurations as with the white parents' group. In this experience, we are sensitive to one another, and we react to one another. We feel loved and approved of, or hated and rejected by others in the group, and this affects our emotional reactions.

Our reactions to others initiate a variety of reactions from them in response. This is the interactive, reciprocal process of the emotional system under the influence of the togetherness force. For example, we may want to please certain others and feel hurt if they are not pleased with us. In that event, if we are angry or disappointed in ourselves for failing to please them, we criticize these others for not doing or being what we want. We become preoccupied with such feelings if we are strongly fused into this emotional system. The white parents' group, at least initially, was consumed by their reactivity. Their level of fusion was very high. They focused on the black community as the cause of their problems and they pushed back.

Our sensitivity to the togetherness force is what allows us to have empathy for others, to feel sorry for them, and to be sad about their circumstances. We identify with them, and sympathize. We share joys and sorrows. Within this reciprocal system, we feel responsible for each other and are more willing to do good on behalf of others. On the other hand, this sensitivity may lead us to do harm. The white teachers had sympathetic feelings for the black community, but their negative reaction to what they perceived as the racism of the white students, was harmful.

The togetherness force also affects our beliefs, opinions, and values. For example, our spiritual beliefs are often quite susceptible to what others who are important to us believe. There is an emotional power and influence at work in the church as we respond to the preachers and teachers and to other leaders who openly express their beliefs. We go along with them, or we rebel against them. If acceptance by group members is the critical issue for us, we modify our beliefs to fit theirs. On the other hand, if we doubt what they say, we may remain quiet about it. Dogmatic and demagogic leaders rely on this conforming reality among people.

Under the influence of the togetherness force, there is a strong push for sameness in feelings, beliefs, thinking, and actions. Unity is expressed in this sameness. In more rigidly fused systems, differences may not be tolerated. The white parents' group expected unanimity of attitudes among its members, even though not all members had the same degree of racist beliefs. No one challenged or spoke out about these differences. They all acted as if they believed the same things.

At its best, the togetherness force brings enjoyment and the experience of mutuality. We are attracted to someone; we fall in love, and we choose to spend our lives together. We want to have children and enjoy their growth into adulthood. It is pleasurable and pleasant to share these mutual experiences. It is the joy of singing, dancing, and playing together, of cheering for our team or our country or our side. This force creates and helps maintain our social lives. Fortunately, it also allowed the white parents, eventually, to connect with the black parents and find some social comfort in that, in spite of their racial attitudes.

The individuality force is also deeply rooted in human nature. It stimulates us to grow and develop physically, intellectually, and emotionally. It is what leads us to create our own sense of self, to become a separate, unique individual. It feeds our creativity, and it pushes us to strive in some way, to express our identities and what makes sense to us. Under its influence, we develop varying degrees of independence, along with the ability to think our own thoughts, develop our own beliefs and opinions, and to be less directed by others. The individuality force impels us to grow up and assume our own unique identity. When, in any particular situation, others tell us what we should think or feel or do, our individuality may say, "Wait a minute, I need to decide about this on my own."

At lower levels of emotional maturity, togetherness is experienced as more of a need for unity as sameness. There is a belief that to be close, people have to be similar. There is little room for individuality. It is less acceptable for people to have their own separate thoughts and wishes. In times of crisis, when the level of threat is high, the push for unity of thinking, feelings, and action is extremely strong. We often see this in times of national crisis, as in wartime. People who do not agree that the enemy is an evil we must overcome are often considered traitors. Early in the meetings with the white parents, it would not have worked for me to say, "Black people are not your enemy."

What I am here calling emotional maturity is what Bowen theory calls "differentiation of self." I will say more about this differentiation in the fourth chapter. For now, we need to understand that differentiation is supported and helped by the force for individuality. We all differentiate to some degree as we express our individuality in life.

My individuality allowed me to think about a new way to approach racially divisive issues. It was hard for me that my liberal friends and colleagues did not agree with me (togetherness force) on the importance of relating to and working with this group of white parents. My friends and colleagues made it clear that I was not one of them. My individuality allowed me to hang on to my own principles and commitments and not give in to their attempts to dissuade me. In terms of the togetherness force, I felt somewhat sad and definitely alone. Nevertheless, because of my individuality force, I believed in what I was doing and that commitment paid off. Without being too immodest, I believe that, in part because my individuality force was stronger than the togetherness force, I affected a significant part of the whole city, and people's lives improved.

The individuality force impels us to explore new ways of doing things, or to do them in our own way. Usually, when there is a low level of intensity in the emotional system, others do not have a problem with our individuality. They may enjoy it or even celebrate it by giving awards, from simple certificates of recognition to the Nobel prizes, for the work that distinguishes us as individuals.

As the level of emotional maturity in people declines, balancing the two life forces looks more impossible and there is a bigger struggle in doing so. More mature people—those who are well-differentiated—do not experience the two forces in such oppositional terms and accept the need to satisfy both forces in a relationship. For example, in less emotionally mature couples, especially during tense times, there is a strong need for the other to be the same as self—perhaps even in all aspects of life. Couples experiencing these issues often came for counseling saying, "We are just too different." I always knew the problem was not their "differentness." It was their emotional sensitivity to each other within the togetherness force. More emotionally mature couples find ways to be close to each other while maintaining their individual differences, even during times of stress and anxiety. Difference is less of a problem for them. Eventually the black and white parents' groups found a way to do this also.

Anxiety

The main problem in relationships is not that there are differences. What matters is the level of anxiety people bring to the encounter they have around their differences. Those with higher levels of anxiety will have more difficulties and more sensitivity to each other. They will struggle with the differences and there will be more polarization.

Anxiety is defined as the experience of threat, whether real or imagined. Real threat, also called acute anxiety, is about some danger that is imminent, possibly life threatening, as when very real flood or tornado warnings are in effect. In a riot situation, a real threat is getting beaten up, or knifed, or shot by an opponent. Imagined threats, also called chronic anxiety, are real to the person experiencing them, but most often they are distant and not even very likely to happen (like fearing every rainstorm will lead to a flood). When emotional systems get out of balance, it is normal for there to be some degree of anxiety. Any lack of balance in a system can create a sense of threat.

Whenever there is a sense of threat, whether it is real or imagined, we become anxious. We are not always clear about the origin of our sense of threat. A certain number of people have greater difficulty discriminating between a real and an imagined threat. For example, claustrophobics cannot explain why, in small spaces, they have a sense that the walls are closing in on them, but the threat is real enough for them to use the stairs rather than an elevator. Rationally, they know the walls will not collapse on them but that does not reduce the intensity of the anxiety.

Anxiety is a very uncomfortable experience. When we feel it, we immediately look for its cause and try to eliminate it, but it is not that simple. Under the influence of anxiety, it is difficult to think in systematic ways. We focus on specific parts of the system as a problem. We tend to think in terms of direct cause and effect. We think, for example, that other people (like an acting-out adolescent) cause our anxiety, and we react to these people rather than examining our own feelings.

Anxiety is socially contagious. It moves through an emotional system separately from the initial stimulus. People who listen to talk radio (on the left as well as the right) experience anxiety about threats they would never imagine until they hear some passionate speaker expound on it. Then they are caught up in the reactivity through the influence of the togetherness force. Anxiety passes from group to group and from one generation to another. It moves horizontally across cultures and vertically through time. Look at the impact of the Great Depression on the children of the parents who experienced it.

The onset of anxiety provokes physiological and psychological changes in a person. We call it stress. Chronic anxiety also affects a person's psychological well-being, and, if it persists over time, it affects their biological functioning as well. It causes wariness, guardedness, suspicion, tension, more susceptibility to stress, as well as physical symptoms. It wears away at us. We are less resilient in our responses to acute anxiety from the normal stresses of life, and this keeps us, as we say, "more on edge." It impedes our ability to think, to be flexible, and to function effectively.

People on both sides of the riot situation were deeply influenced by their anxieties, both acute and chronic. Some were more anxious than others, but in all cases, their anxiety stimulated them to act. During the riot itself, some ran away and hid while others aggressively engaged in direct fighting with "the enemy." Few of them thought clearly about the situation in broader, more systematic terms.

Church communities are susceptible to chronic anxiety; factors that affect the spread of anxiety in a congregation include:

- the severity and magnitude of the stressor;
- the degree of perceived threat;
- the state and condition of the relationship network in the church;
- the average level of fusion of the group members; and
- the ability of leaders to act in a more mature and non-reactive manner in the face of pressures that are feeding the anxiety.

In chapter six, I tell the story of a church that handled this anxiety well.

When just one leader can better manage his or her own anxiety, staying well connected emotionally to the others in the church, in particular to key leaders, it has a calming effect on the larger system. With both an anxious congregation and anxious leaders, difficulties develop. For example, it is normal to be anxious and reactive when a leader in the church is angry with us. We get defensive and make excuses, or struggle and fight back, trying to win the argument and prove we are right. Or we choose to yield rather than to argue, but that can lead to resentment on our part. Another choice, however, is to move toward this person with interest, demonstrating that we understand and appreciate the energy and concern he or she has expressed and that we are willing to explore the issue. My low level of anxiety and reactivity with the white parents, as I moved toward them with interest in what they had to say, eventually helped them to be less reactive and more thoughtful themselves.

Bowen family systems theory

There are eight specific and interlocking concepts in the Bowen theory. The understanding of emotional systems, the life forces of togetherness and individuality, and anxiety all function within and through these eight concepts. They are:

- nuclear family emotional system,
- projection to a child,
- triangles and interlocking triangles,
- differentiation of self,
- sibling position,
- emotional cutoff,
- multigenerational transmission process, and
- emotional process in society.

Dr. Bowen's theory developed first within the context of his research on and psychotherapy with families that had an alcoholic member, and, later, one that had a schizophrenic member. He generalized his theory to all families including his own. He recognized that his theory described relationships at the societal level, as well as the smaller, family group level. Finally, he added the emotional process in society to his theory. He saw that the theory describes how social groups (including organizations like the church) grow healthier over time or become more regressive and reactionary. I will say more about this concept in the fifth chapter.

A focus on the functional facts of emotional relationships is quite different from the usual approach of psychotherapy, which focuses on what people say about their experiences, especially regarding their feelings. Bowen theory does not rely on peoples' subjective reports of what they feel in relationships. It is more about what they actually do. For example, sports commentators have many opinions about the sports they cover, but there is opinion and then there is actual play on the field. In psychotherapy, it is easy to confuse the two. It is the play on the field that counts. Bowen theory focuses on the actual play, not on the commentary by people with opinions, like counselors, about the psychological meaning of the play.

Part of the genius of his theory is that it offers a way to be more objective about the highly subjective experience of emotional relationships. It does this, in part, by focusing on the who, where, what, when, and how of relationships rather than on what people say about why they do what they do, or why they feel what they feel. It avoids the cause/effect thinking that "why" questions inevitably involve us in.

Nuclear family emotional system

This concept describes the automatic emotional process that happens in any family (or social group) given enough stress and anxiety when differences arise. The husband and wife function in reciprocal response to one another. How intensely they do this depends on their level of fusion. When their level of anxiety exceeds their ability to manage it within a direct face-to-face, one-on-one relationship where they openly communicate their concerns to one another, then they resort to one or more of four predictable behavioral mechanisms for managing their anxiety:

- compliance
- marital conflict
- projection to a child
- emotional distancing

Compliance: Rather than work directly and openly about differences with the partner, one gives up self to the other, refuses to address their differences, and complies (more or less) with the partner's expectations. This usually leads to a pattern of over- and underfunctioning. One partner, either husband or wife, assumes the role of the dominant one, the authority that dictates what is to be done, or in the guise of a more caring person, the one who simply tells people what they need to do or "should" do. The way this is carried out takes many different forms.

Overfunctioning involves taking responsibility for others. It means doing their thinking for them, deciding for them, and perhaps even acting for them. The underfunctioner gives up his or her autonomy and individuality, including the ability to think and act as a separate person, and goes along with whatever is proposed, often without much objection.

Another way this mechanism displays itself is that one of the partners, usually the more compliant one, develops a physical, emotional, or social symptom. A severe addiction—say to alcohol—is an example that involves all three of these symptoms. The alcoholic eventually develops physical problems related to alcohol abuse, along with emotional problems like depression. In addition, the alcoholic might have, at some point, an encounter with the police and the courts, thus having a social symptom. Issues multiply, then, as the alcoholic encounters systems outside the family, including the medical, psychological, and legal systems. As a rule, these outside systems focus on drinking as the problem rather than looking into the emotional system of the alcoholic. If things do not change in the family emotional system, the alcoholic's situation is likely to get worse, even if he or she goes to Alcoholics Anonymous and "sobers up." In fact, most divorces occur after the problem drinker has sobered up.

Marital conflict: Unlike compliance, in this case, the partners' differences are out in the open but they cannot come to any agreement concerning them. Compromise is out of the question because it feels like a loss of self to the other. Perhaps the open conflict is a cover for deeper issues they do not want to address.

This conflict is usually a battle of who knows best, with each telling the other, "You are wrong, and I am right," and that things should be done "my way." Or one person rebels against the other, saying something like, "You can't tell me what to do. I will do whatever I want to do." In both cases, the opposition is out in the open and powerfully expressed through fighting, possibly leading to physical violence. Either way, each partner seeks to control the thinking and feelings of the other through the reactive process. They each get cues for how to act from the other's actions. They are focused on what the other says and does, and that determines how self will be. The sarcastic and sometimes vicious arguments of George and Martha, characters in Edward Albee's play *Who's Afraid of Virginia Woolf?*, provide a perfect example of such an intense conflict, demonstrating how couples like this would rather argue than address underlying issues.

Projection to a child: Initially described as one of the mechanisms used to manage anxiety in the family, Bowen later decided that this process was so important and pervasive that it should be a separate concept. I explore this concept in the next sub-section, and it is further described in the chapter on triangles.

Emotional distancing: This mechanism is actually central to the other three, and it is the most common mechanism for us all. Everyone does it regularly to some extent. In emotional distancing, we refuse to engage with others regarding important issues in the relationship. We ignore the importance of these issues or we just send a message, in sometimes subtle ways, that we are not going to deal with it. When we go silent in a relationship, or become non-responsive in some way, we are refusing to engage and we we are distancing emotionally. A husband chooses to read the paper or watch TV, or he engages in a hobby instead of talking with his wife; a child stays engrossed in a computer game rather than listening to a parent. Walking out of the room when the other enters, takes it to the physical realm. Emotional distancing is present in the other mechanisms because each person is refusing to be open about self or to demonstrate interest in the thoughts of the other. We have all probably done this with our own parents.

Projection to a child

When a family system experiences a certain amount of anxiety around differences, one solution to the uneasiness is to focus on one (or more) child's (perhaps normal) developmental problems. Parents typically diagnose and try to fix that child's behavior. This process usually begins with an unresolved issue between the husband and wife that they cannot address adequately. It is easier for them to focus on a child. Other family members (like a sibling or grandparent) can be recruited into the process. The family members put their emotional energy into this effort to "fix" the child. The more they project their anxiety on to the child (with the intention of trying to help the child do better), the worse the child's problems or behaviors become. The next step is to take the child to a counselor saying, in effect, "This child is the problem in our family. He (or she) is keeping us from being a happy family." If the counselor does not use a family systems theory approach, then he or she accepts this definition of the problem and joins the family in trying to fix the child, ignoring the larger issue of anxiety in the family.

The triangle and interlocking triangles

The concept of triangles illustrates how we typically live our lives in relationships. For example, we often consider people who share our views of others to be our friends. We join with our friends against those who differ from us. Together, my friend and I form a close twosome against a third person who is on the outside of our relationship. The third person does not have to be an enemy, just someone we might consider "too different" (perhaps in behaviors or beliefs) to be one of us. Refusing to engage in triangles is one way we can interrupt the process. The Good Samaritan did not say, "Oh, this man is a Jew. He is not of my faith. I should not help him." He saw a man in need and cared for him. It was a direct one-to-one relationship. Chapter three deals extensively with the concept of triangles and how they are the basic structure of the polarizing process.

Differentiation of self

Differentiation of self is central concept in Bowen theory because it is the critical element in making a difference in our relationships. It describes the essential personal strength, and sometimes courage, that is required to set things in a new direction rather than, for example, to go with the flow of what all of our friends say is best. The well-differentiated Good

Samaritan may have had to suffer criticism from his friends for helping "the enemy." This concept is so important and so central to the change process that I address it more fully in the fourth chapter.

Multigenerational transmission process

This concept describes how anxiety and unresolved emotional attachment issues in a family system can be passed down from one generation of the family to another. Each nuclear family has a certain amount of unresolved emotional attachment, which will generate anxiety in the larger family system. This anxiety exists primarily in the parental subsystem (not as the cause, but resident within the two parents and reflected in their relationship). Their anxiety is transmitted, in variable ways, to their children, with some getting more and some less.

When the children in this kind of family situation grow up, they carry into their new relationships the level of emotional maturity (differentiation of self) they developed in their original family. Moreover, they also bring a level of chronic anxiety from their family of origin. This anxiety is acted out through one or more of the four behavioral mechanisms (compliance, marital conflict, projection to a child, emotional distancing) in their new nuclear family emotional system. This perpetuates the anxiety related to unresolved emotional attachment in succeeding generations.

To the extent that there is a relatively mature (well-differentiated) couple to start with, and, if whatever chronic anxiety they have is not projected on to one or more of the children, succeeding generations are likely to gradually improve their level of emotional maturity. When a child is selected for the projection process, then that child has higher anxiety and a lower level of maturity. He or she may marry someone at the same level, and if the spouse's parents also engaged in the projection process, the succeeding generations will move lower and lower in their levels of differentiation.

Ronald W. Richardson

Sibling position

This is the one concept that Bowen adopted from someone else. The psychologist Walter Toman (1993) described how children in various sibling positions develop differently from one another within their family. These insights helped Bowen focus his own thinking about families as systems. Toman did research on many thousands of non-clinical couples on two continents and discovered predictable personality and behavioral variations between them based on their sibling position in the family.

Toman (1993) identified ten sibling positions that influence how children develop into adults. He gives the characteristics that tend to be true of each one as a result of birth order, whether they were male or female, and if each had male or female siblings. I have taken the liberty of dividing his ninth category (only child) to specify gender, as different dynamics may be at work regarding the gender of the only child. Here is my adaptation of Toman's categories:

- Older brother of brothers
- Older brother of sisters
- Older sister of sisters
- Older sister of brothers
- Youngest brother of brothers
- Youngest brother of sisters
- Youngest sister of sisters
- Youngest brother of sisters
- Only male child
- Only female child, and
- Twins. (Middle children are some mixture of the other positions.)

Older brothers of brothers function in their adult relationships differently from older brothers of sisters. Youngest sisters of sisters function differently from youngest sisters of brothers. Moreover, when these people marry each other they develop different kinds of marriages from those of their siblings.

In my clinical practice, I found Toman's descriptions to be generally accurate. When they were not, Bowen's additions to Toman's work clarified for me why a person did not fit the description of their sibling position. This information helped me lead many of my clients to a new understanding of their marital relationship, their parents' way of functioning, and the differences between their children. People who work together in the same office have found the sibling information to be helpful in their working relationships. Lois and I, both only children, found Toman's work revelatory in helping us to understand some of the difficulties we experienced in our marriage.

Emotional cutoff

This concept is an extension of Bowen's understanding of emotional distancing, but it differs in that it is applied primarily to distance between the generations. When I moved away from home as a young man, I physically extended a significant emotional distance (a cutoff) from my mother. I began the cutoff long before I left home. I contacted her only on her birthday and at Christmas, and she rarely knew what I was doing. I gave much of the history of this relationship, and how I dealt with it over time, in a previous book, *Becoming a Healthier Pastor* (2004). People often put some distance between themselves and their parents, believing that, in doing so they can be free of their parents' problems or intrusions in their lives.

I had the pleasure of hearing Bowen speak at a conference in Vancouver, where he reminded us that "time and distance do not fool an emotional system." The unresolved emotional attachments in our family of origin, maintained by emotional cutoff, transmit to new adult relationships. Such unresolved attachments can affect not only our marriages and parenting skills, but also our friendships, our lives in our workplace, our relationships with our church, and our behaviors in society. They create in us a sensitivity that goes with us into our adult lives. If, for example, a person always feels greatly disrespected in his or her family of origin, he or she develops a kind of radar that presumes a lack of respect in others, whether that disrespect is real or imagined. The person feels it as a threat to self's well-being, and then reacts to it with the same kind of vehemence he or she felt in the family of origin.

Emotional cutoff does not require physical distance. One can be living in the same house with one's parents and still be quite cut off from them. Great distances between a husband and wife with little or no emotional contact are not uncommon. In this case, the phenomenon is called emotional divorce.

Paradoxically, adult fusion with the family of origin can be expressed either by never leaving home or by rarely having contact with family after leaving. Most people do some version between the two. Bowen said, "The person who runs away from home is as emotionally attached as the one who stays at home and uses internal mechanisms to control the attachment. The one who runs away has a different life course. He needs emotional closeness but is allergic to it. He runs away, kidding himself that he is achieving 'independence.' The more intense the cutoff with his parents, the more he is vulnerable to repeating the same pattern in future relationships" (535).

Emotional process in society

This last concept in Bowen's theory is the topic of this book. He was able to show that very similar kinds of emotional processes are at work at both the family and the societal level. Anxiety in society transmits in much the same way as in families. Just as families can go into a regressive process through the generations, so can societies.

Conclusion

My work with the white parents' group, and what it eventually led to, is one example of societal progression rather than regression. The white and black parents were able to overcome the regressive elements in their immediate society and work together toward some mutual ideas about their children's education and how to achieve their goals. However, together, we could not adequately address the sources of anxiety that originated beyond our small community. The fifth chapter provides a more detailed description of the concept of emotional process in society.

3

The Triangle and Polarization in Family, Church, and Society

What is a triangle?

Triangles contribute to the polarization process. If you do not know what I mean by the word "triangle," I can assure you that you directly experience them on a daily basis, perhaps many times a day. They are critical to your functioning in relationships. Triangles are a basic part of church life, just as they are in our family and in our social life generally. Each one of us is involved in many ongoing triangles. They are powerful and pervasive.

At the mention of the word triangle, some people think of the classic one of a husband with a wife and a mistress. We are all aware of famous leaders, throughout history, who have presented us with such painful, and yet tantalizing, stories of triangular life. They have become a form of entertainment in our media. These kinds of stories have been going on since human beings first inhabited the earth, and I can just imagine early cave people gossiping about the clan chieftain and, "who he is sleeping with now."

A triangle typically has two people in the inside position, who are called the "close twosome," and one in the outside position. The person in the outside position is usually more distant from the other two, even if only for a brief time. When things are calm between the close twosome, the outside person may devise strategies to get in and be close to one (or both). For example, when mom and dad hug, it is quite normal to see a young child run over to them and try to get in between them, usually to hug mom. During tense times between the close twosome, the outside person is usually happy to be outside, unless that person thinks he or she can rescue the one who appears to be the victim, and thus affirm greater closeness with that person. Thus, the outside person joins a close twosome, while the other moves to the outside. Membership in triangles often moves dynamically in such a fashion, with members shifting from the inside to the outside and back again.

Two parents talking about one of their children out of concern for that child exemplify a common family triangle. In the church, it could be a parishioner and a pastor talking about the parishioner's spouse. They agree that he or she has a problem and they ponder what to do about it. It could be two parishioners talking about what they like or dislike about their pastor.

When someone in the church starts telling you a negative story about someone else in the church, then you are in a triangle. In telling you the story, that person expects you to agree, as if you are part of the close twosome. The absent person is in the outside position. If you agree, the two of you will probably keep telling each other negative stories about this third person, building a case against him or her, offering each other further proof of how wrong or bad that third person is.

If you do not agree with the speaker and say so, the person telling you the negative story will probably pull away and go to someone else with the story. However, that will not end your part in that triangling process, you will just be in the outside position along with the person being talked about. You will become one of "them" rather than one of "us." The speaker may even talk about you and say that you agree (whether you do or not). Whenever two people communicate about a third who is absent, that is a triangle. They do not have to speak. The closeness could be affirmed simply in a glance they give each other when the third person enters the room.

In addition, triangles are not always restricted to just three people. The race riot situation was full of triangles, but a basic one was the white people (parents and students), the black people (parents and students), and the school system (teachers and administrators). The white people felt like they were in the outside position and that the black people and school system were the close twosome. The white people were viewed negatively because of their obvious racism. Historically, the white people had been on the inside position with the schools and the blacks were outside, with no influence on school administration or curriculum. Now the triangular positions had shifted.

A common church triangle occurs when we use Jesus or Paul to bolster our own ideas and opinions, quoting Biblical scripture as a means of defending our ideas. I could act as if Jesus and I are the close twosome as "we" address the others. We preachers often do this. Jesus does not have a chance to differentiate himself from me. Of course, some of those whom I address may believe that they walk more closely with Jesus than I, or that they know him better than I, and that he is on their side when they quote him back to me. We all play this game. We do it in our polarizing church fights. Our list of triangular options in the church is endless.

The origin of triangles

Murray Bowen called triangles the basic molecule, or building block, of emotional systems. If we think of individual people as the atoms in an emotional system, then the grouping of three (or more) people around some relational difficulty is the molecule. Bowen tells us that the two person dyadic relationship is unstable. He means that it is difficult for any two people to keep their focus just on themselves in a one-to-one relationship as they relate to one another. At some point, when there is some degree of increased tension, they will be more comfortable talking about a third person or an issue rather than addressing the source of the tension between them.

In a one-to-one relationship, you and I talk with each other only about you or me or our relationship. The more mature or differentiated we each are, the better we can maintain that one-to-one relationship even in times of high anxiety. This one-to-one relationship is, in fact, relatively rare even in our closest relationships.

More typically, when talking with those we are "close to," we talk about others, or situations, or issues, and so forth. Friends tell each other stories about other people they know. One classic family triangle is that of mother, a problematic child, and father. When there is an emotional divorce between the parents, dad is usually in the outside position and, in those cases, he may be called weak, passive, and distant. The mother may be called aggressive, dominating, and even castrating. As they argue and struggle to decide what to do about their problematic child, the child may slip further into chronic functional impairment due to the projection process. However, this very process may serve to stabilize the parental relationship as they focus on the child.

The close/distant dance

We each have variable comfort zones around closeness and distance with the people who are emotionally important to us. If you are an important person in my life, like my mother or my partner, I might, at some point, begin to feel like you are "too close." You may want to know some particular thing about me that I feel uncomfortable talking about with you. Alternatively, you may start telling me what you think I should think, or feel, or do after I have revealed something about myself to you. As this happens, at some point, I start backing away out of fear of being absorbed by you or losing myself in you; I might feel overwhelmed by you, thinking you are trying to change me somehow. As I back away emotionally, you may come at me more strongly with your argument.

This is the emotional pursue/distance pattern that is common in relationships. There is implicit (if not explicit) pressure for me to become like you, to see life the way you want me to. I may think my individuality is threatened. This is, for example, a typical parent/adolescent conflict with the parent telling the teenager how to run his or her life. Every parent recognizes this experience. We did it ourselves as teens. Consequently, the teen distances from the parents and moves closer to peers.

Here is an example of a typical close/distant interaction between a husband and wife. Out of some anxiety of her own, the wife begins the pursuit around a topic or relationship issue that the husband finds uncomfortable, so he distances. He might go beyond just concentrating on reading the paper or watching sports on TV; he might create physical distance by going to the golf course or to "men's night out" every chance he gets.

After some period of pursuit, feeling cut off and as if she has run into a stone wall, the wife gives up, saying she cannot get through to him. (Just remember you pursuers, a distancer can always outdistance a pursuer.) After enough experiences of this sort, and often in a mix of despair and anger, she reacts by distancing from him. When this happens often enough, she may begin to have fantasies of leaving the marriage, even make actual plans to do so.

At that point the husband often senses this and begins to feel anxious about the distance. He begins to fear that if he moves too far away he might be abandoned and left alone. Therefore, in the third stage he becomes the pursuer, saying, "I'm sorry. I'll do better. Please don't leave." Depending on how bitter she is, she may respond to this overture and then the equilibrium between them will be reestablished for some period. Later, at some point, it is likely the process will repeat all over again.

I have a friend whose husband died. She loved him but her big complaint was that he never talked. She was especially interested in what he was feeling. She would pursue and pursue, but he always outdistanced her. After his death, when she was ready to remarry, the main qualities she wanted in a man were warmth, sensitivity, and a willingness to talk to her. And she found one. But it did not take long into the marriage for her to try to get away from him. She said, "All he wants to do is talk. About feelings and everything. I can't stand it. He is so intrusive. He needs me too much. I need time and space on my own." She sounded like a lot of men and now she says, "I see how my first husband felt." She can see the irony.

We have many opportunities for emotional distancing in the church, but a common time is during the pastor's sermon when we simply pull a shade down over our eyes, figuratively cover our ears and smile and nod our heads as if we agree. We are keeping the peace. We are not engaging in the issue. On the other hand, the extent that I, as your pastor, come off as a parent in the pulpit, telling you how to live your life is the extent that I am likely to evoke some form of adolescent rebellion and, perhaps, emotional distancing by you and others in the pews. Pursuers and distancers go hand in hand. You cannot have one without the other.

Close/distant dance and triangles

This close/distant dance is one way triangles start. Anxiety is the issue that gets us either to distance from or to pursue one another. It is anxiety over incorporation into or inundation by the other (as in the case of distancing) or abandonment by the other (as in the case of pursuing). It is about being too close or too far apart. When I distance, I do not just distance from you. I also move toward someone or something else. For some people this may be their job. However, it could be a group of friends, a particular friend, an affair, a hobby, TV, a sport like golf, or something else—anything that increases the distance.

When my friend started distancing from her new husband, she decided to become an artist, and, over the years, she has done very well with it. She spends a lot of time with other artists in her community and less time with him. Now her art is the "good" reason she has less time to sit and talk with him.

Initially, he resented her art and her new friends because they took her away from him. Distancers move toward someone or something else, where they usually feel more comfortable, perhaps more competent, and less anxious, and that creates the third corner in a triangle. My friend's husband was wise enough not to pursue her. Instead, he took a volunteer job that met some of his needs for closeness; it has worked for both of them.

Pursuers can also initiate triangles. When they are not getting what they want from the object of their pursuit, they often recruit a third person to help them. This could be another person like a friend, a counselor, or a pastor. If the husband has a problem of some sort, like drinking, the wife may try to get the pastor to help her "fix" him. The wife pursues the pastor, to form a triangle, so they both, as the close twosome, can focus on and "fix" the husband. If the pastor joins in this triangle, then the husband will also start distancing from him.

If the pastor does not feel comfortable handling a marital issue of this sort, he may distance from the wife. Then the wife may tell a good friend how "useless" the pastor was in helping her. The friend may then tell others that the pastor is not competent to give pastoral care. On it will go.

Fluid or fixed triangles

Triangles may be fluid or fixed. Here is an example of the basic fluid triangle where the person in the close twosome shifts around: two people in the triangle appear to be close, perhaps Jim and me. We relate to each other about a third person, Harry, who appears, at the time, to be the more distant outsider. Jim and I talk about Harry and "his problem." It does not have to be intentionally malicious talk; we could just be concerned. We act as if we were close because of our agreement about him.

Then, Jim and Harry meet, and they talk about me and act as if they agree about me and what they see as my problem. However, Jim does not tell Harry what he said to me about

Harry. Nor does Jim tell me what he told Harry about me. They get their apparent closeness by talking about me.

Later, Harry and I get together and we talk about Jim. Neither of us tells the other what we have said to Jim, and we act as if we agree in our mutual evaluation of Jim. If Jim walks up to us while Harry and I are talking about him, we immediately change the subject to something else; Jim may notice and find himself feeling funny and wondering what is going on. In triangles like this, people never know where they stand with others. People are not direct with each other. There is generally lots of confusion about what is going on in a relationship.

Here are two principles to remember about triangles: first, if you feel frequently confused about what is going on in a relationship, you might be in a triangle. What triangles might you be unaware of? Try to identify them so you can begin to deal productively with them. The second principle is that if someone talks with you in this triangular manner about someone else, then it is likely you are the subject of similar talk behind your back. I can almost guarantee this.

The basic fixed triangle

There are also fixed triangles where the close twosome and the person in the outside position remain the same over time. We are each born into a new triangle in our families as infants. We grow up into adulthood living constantly within that triangle. "Mom, dad, and me" is the first, and usually the most powerful, triangle in our lives. Normally, not always, it is a fixed triangle with us being closer to one parent than the other.

Fixed triangles can last as long as the three characters are alive, and even extend beyond the grave. I have had sixty- and seventy-year-old clients, high-powered, business executives, who are still involved in this basic, fixed, parental triangle, acting as if they are still problematic adolescents. One question I ask clients is, "How long does it take you, in a phone call home, or in a visit to your parents, to get those old adolescent feelings and start reacting like you are in high school again?"

Our functioning in the parental triangle, as growing children, has a great deal to do with how we function in our varied adult social relationships, including our own parenting. This is important, and it is the reason it is essential that, as a pastor, you get to know the people in your church, as well as understanding how you function in your own family.

That primary triangular relationship—mom, dad, and me—in our own families will affect how church members function in their congregational life and relationships, as well as in other emotionally important relationships. We carry those early family relationships and primary triangles around with us as a kind of emotional system—an aura—that affects us as adults. They affect our emotional sensitivities and our attractions and reactions to other people. If we make an effort to get to know more about people and their family experience growing up, we will have more insight into their life with us in the church and we will be more effective in ministering to their needs. My experience with intensely polarized people is that they have intense triangles within their own family of origin. It is a way of life for them.

The one-to-one relationship

A major goal in implementing Bowen theory is to achieve one-to-one relationships with everyone involved in the system, whether it is your family, or your work system, or your faith group. Of course that ideal is not always achievable, but the better we can move toward that goal the better it will be for the system as a whole.

Again, a good one-to-one relationship means I am open with you about whatever I think, feel, and want to do, or have done, and I do not worry about your reaction to that openness. I do not let concern about your reactions keep me from doing something, nor do I think, "You must accept me before I can do this." Equally, I can hear your openness about these things and not have the need to condemn or judge you, or agree with you. Agreement is not the goal.

This is what I mean by intimacy. Not everyone thinks of intimacy in the same way. What some people mean is that, "We are intimate if I can tell you everything I think about other people in my life." This is not intimacy; it is just continuing the triangle as the close twosome. This is the major problem with secrets. They distort relationships.

In terms of preventive measures, building a one-to-one relationship with as many people as possible is one of the most important things a pastor can do for the congregation and the church community. The better you know people in your church and the more you have improved your connection with them, the better the church and its members will be able deal with any crisis that arises. The tendency toward polarization is automatically reduced.

Interlocking triangles and the polarization process

Triangles are an essential part of the polarization process. Pick any hot subject and you immediately see how it works. How about abortion? Feelings run high on both sides and each side sees it as a critical issue. Part of what we do, in maintaining whatever position we have on the topic, is to bolster our side with awful stories about the other side and the horrors they commit. That way we feel more righteous in our own position. We rarely engage in any direct, open, nonconfrontational communication with people on the other side. It feels more comfortable to talk with the people who agree with us and share negative stories about the other side. That is a clear, polarized social triangle.

For Bowen, the concept of the triangle and interlocking triangles in families became the bridge to understanding the social process. Triangles are about trying to manage anxiety in relationships. For example, in consulting with teachers or principals in schools, one can easily observe the functioning of interlocking triangles in society.

Take the issue of a "white racist teenager," or any sort of "problem child." Too often the scenario follows a predictable pattern. His teacher talks with other teachers and with school administrators who agree that he is a problem. Next, they all talk with social workers, or counselors, who take on the project of "fixing" this problem teen. They may or may not talk with his parents. The more they focus on him, the worse his problems seem to be. Then he starts getting into serious fights, assaulting black teens at school. The administration calls the police, which introduces another triangle to the mix. After several police visits, they charge him and he goes to court. The legal system adds another interlocking triangle. A court social worker is called in, but with little effect, and eventually the teen ends up in prison, on his way to being a hardened criminal at odds with society. It may seem like an extreme example, but it illustrates the potential damage that a cascading series of interlocking triangles can do. The beginning of the triangle is in the anxiety of the original dyad—teacher and teen—and if they cannot find a way to directly deal with the issues, then the rest of the process is almost inevitable.

As anxiety moves through the various interlocking triangles focused on this teen, each person loses touch with his or her ability to think more clearly about what is going on and the self's own functioning; rather, it gets more focused on how to control the teen and stop him from being "a problem." All along the way, there are emotionally-based decisions governed by the anxiety of the moment.

Very often, people engaged in polarizing behavior are operating out of their position in the triangles of their family of origin. A social worker trainee in my counselor-training program is a good example of how the family of origin triangle is related to the way a person functions in society. She wanted to protect a female client from the emotional abuse of her husband. Her general attitude of sympathy for and fervently advocating for the less fortunate people in society betrayed the sense that something else was going on. Remember, if confused, think triangles. In my work with her, it became clear that she had played a central role in a triangle with her parents, trying to protect her mother from her father. She criticized him with the same fervor she did about the wrongs of society, but she had had little success in either changing him or her mother. Her stance was her way of dealing with the anxiety that was based, first, within her family, and, later, in her work as a counselor within society.

Another important principle of triangles is that a third person cannot change the relationship between two other people. My staff counselor learned to be interested in the functional patterns of her clients, talking with each one of them about their experience in their relationship with the partner (she also did this with her own parents), and in their own thinking about how they functioned in that relationship. She became less of a rescuer in both systems. This change had an impact in both those systems and in her. She was able to shift her position in the triangles and, thus, become more of a resource for everyone involved, both her clients and her parents.

Neutrality as the way to reduce polarization

A knowledge of triangles is essential to avoiding polarization in the church. Triangles quickly become part of the normal pattern of relating if we are not aware of them. This knowledge offers us a theory-based resource for interrupting the process. Optimistically, as leaders, we can remain a related outsider who can work closely with all of the involved, conflicted members. It is personally hard to achieve this "outside, but connected" position in practice. It is easy for others to involve us emotionally if we are not paying attention. We may be susceptible to their triangular moves. They may say or imply that it is our job as leaders to fix relationships in the church or that it is our job as leaders to take a side in the dispute. We have to ensure that the responsibility remains with those involved in difficult relationships, not allowing them or others to shift the responsibility to us and refusing to let them to tell us what we should do to fix things.

This requires us to learn about maintaining emotional neutrality with any church members in triangular situations. The personal skills we need for this are outlined in the next chapter on differentiation of self. Making this sort of effort in our own family of origin is a good first step. If we can wade into the emotional turmoil that exists within our own family life, relate equally well with all of our family members, and not take sides around who is right and who is wrong, then we are better equipped to do this in the church. Our family of origin is the best training ground for this effort since emotionality often runs quite high in families.

In the church, if we can manage self well enough, staying in what is called "viable emotional contact" with all parties, and remaining outside the emotional activity of a central triangle, then conflict is more manageable and things will get better. The fusion between the two sides will slowly begin to resolve, and all other church members will benefit as they change in relation to each other. This is the basic theory and method for reducing polarization in the church, or any other social group. I will say more about this in chapter nine. It is not easy, but it works almost like magic.

In general, the more intense the fusion and the higher the anxiety, the longer any issue will take to resolve. Although the other members may be angry with you for not taking a side, they will greatly appreciate it in the end. For you, as a leader, taking a side will only intensify the polarizing process and will not resolve anything.

When tensions have run very high in churches, a split begins to materialize. Outside groups may become involved (creating interlocking triangles), and they are asked to take a side. Eventually the denomination is involved, and maybe even the police or the courts. The more this occurs, the more upsetting and destructive, and perhaps irredeemable, it will be.

It is most helpful to focus on the central triangle in the church in order to modify this process. If this central triangle has a reduced intensity, then others related to it will also calm down. It requires some study of the emotional process in your church, tracking who does what, when, and how, so that things do not escalate. In this way, we can discover the central triangle. If just one of the participants begins to think more about self's part in the process, reacts less, and more clearly thinks through the self's own position, then the intensity is lessened. This begins with you as a leader.

There are many intricacies to this process, but there are a few simple ideas about maintaining emotional neutrality. The key is being able to stay interested in and emotionally connected with both sides of a triangle without taking sides. By the way, simply telling people, "I don't take sides" will not change things. I encourage you not to say things like this. It only puts people off. It helps you feel better, but it does not promote change.

Staying emotionally connected with both sides involves being curious, asking questions, clarifying facts and the thinking behind people's behavior, and hearing about feelings without focusing on them. Your interest helps those involved to think about their part in the process. They make rational-sounding arguments and emotional appeals and tell stories about the other side. All of this is designed to bring you over to their side. If you listen to the content of all of this, without thinking about what it is designed to do (involve you in the triangle), then you are lost. Taking sides in whatever stories they tell, no matter how reasonable or right they sound, keeps triangles going. Side taking is such a subtle process you may not even realize you are doing it. Giving advice is one way of taking a side. What is often called "being supportive" is another.

Emotional neutrality means neither approving nor disapproving of other people and their attitudes or behavior. This is what I had to do with the white parents' group. It is not about being wishy-washy yourself. I knew where I stood personally with regard to racism (it would have been easy to take a side), but I was not about to interject my own beliefs into the argument. You can have your own beliefs (focused on what you would or would not do in a situation, not what you think they should do) and still be neutral. I was able to avoid judging either side. I remained focused on facts, hearing and accepting feelings but not focusing on them. For example, I would never ask, "How did you feel about that?"

If we see them as either victims or victimizers when people tell us their stories about being upset with others, then we are probably in the triangular role of rescuer or savior. We have to see past these symptoms. We need to find a way to push the triangling person back toward the person with whom they are having the problem. This is part of what happened when we began the interracial parent groups and when we had direct meetings with the school board.

Conclusion

If you are being sympathetic, feeling guilty, assuming responsibility, getting angry with someone, or getting frustrated in hearing someone's story, then you are you are in a triangle. Having any of these feelings means you are not being neutral. You are not helpful. You are part of the problem. Most of these feelings occur when we are in a polarized situation. Feelings change when we change our position in the system.

Repositioning yourself in a neutral way within triangles is not easy. It requires a well-differentiated person. Everyone you meet introduces another potential triangle. This is how people try to solve their problems in life. This is normal. We do it ourselves. How you respond makes all the difference in how the relationship develops. Your response determines whether you will be a resource to the people involved or further contribute to the problems. The next chapter focuses on the personal resource of differentiation of self.

4

Differentiation of Self and Polarization

Differentiation of self and change in the social system

This chapter explores what it takes for leaders to create change in an emotional system in order to reduce the level of polarization within the church so that it can become healthier. The primary variable between individuals, the way they differ from each other in terms of emotional functioning, is their level of differentiation. Those at lower levels and at higher levels, in general, behave quite differently from each other in their life and relationships. This is not about political attitudes and beliefs.

Differentiation is the ability to function more as a separate, autonomous self and be guided less by other people in the emotional system. We differentiate a self out of the emotional fusion of the system. This does not mean emotionally distancing from others. It is about a different way of being with them.

Progress in society depends on people achieving a higher level of differentiation, which comes about because of our change in self and in our relationships. Working toward this goal was the primary focus of my work with the white parents' group. It was critical to my ability to work with them and to bringing about a degree of change. I did not have a name for this process at the time, but I did have some sense of how I had to be present with them.

Bowen theory offers a simple formulation for change. When individuals can better differentiate a self and maintain a good emotional connection with the group they are a part of, change happens. However, we do not differentiate a self in order to change others. Rather, we do it for self. Each person is part of a larger interconnected emotional system and functions as a part of that system. If one person changes the way self functions within that system, maintains this new way of functioning, and refuses to yield to the likely pressure from others to go back to the old way of functioning, then the others will have to adjust. It is a simple idea, but not an easy one to fulfill personally.

Pseudo and solid selves

Bowen's term "pseudo self" refers to that part of us that participates in fusion with others. The pseudo self is pliable. It is not solid. It is the part of self that is reactive to emotional pressure from others (to change thinking, feelings, or behavior) and gives in to the pressure to conform, or, conversely, expects others to conform, or rebels against them. It is composed of the beliefs, opinions, and principles that have been adopted from important others.

Everyone in a system has a certain degree of pseudo self, depending on their level of differentiation. As part of the fusion process, they can trade self back and forth; they can give up self to others, or they can expect others to give up self to them. We defer to others or expect them to defer to us. We change self to make them happy with us, to gain their approval, or to avoid their criticism. Most of us have more pseudo self than we are willing to admit or, more likely, are aware of.

Bowen (1978) said the solid self is composed of the "clearly defined beliefs, opinions, convictions and life principles on which self will take action even in situations of high anxiety and duress" (365). The solid self refers to "who I am; what I believe; what I stand for; and what I will do or not do in a given situation" (365). These beliefs and stances are the result of a process of thinking over time. This more solid self reveals itself in our actions, especially in critical times when others around us are highly anxious.

For example, churches can vary by how much they expect others to go along with the party line, that is, with their orthodox version of faith that the church, or its leaders, presents. The extent to which people conform to those expectations, without thinking their beliefs through for themselves, is the extent to which a church is composed of pseudo selves.

The two foci of differentiation

Differentiation of self has two primary foci. One focus is on the feeling and thinking processes within a person. The second focus is on the person's relationships with others. Looking inward, people vary as to how much fusion there is between their thinking and feelings, and, looking outward, how emotionally fused they are with others.

Feeling and thinking within self

Bowen (1978) said, "The core of my theory has to do with the degree to which people are able to distinguish between the feeling process and the intellectual process" (355). People who have the greatest fusion between these two ways of dealing with the world do the least well in living their lives. They have the highest percentage of life problems. Those who are able to distinguish a feeling from a thought and are able to choose which one they will act upon at any particular time generally do the best in life. They will have the greatest flexibility and adaptability in dealing with the stresses and challenges of life.

The distinction between thinking and feeling is not pejorative. Thinking is not better than feeling. We all necessarily do both, but they are different processes. When we are functioning as more mature people, we can distinguish between them and decide how to act. In the large group meetings with hundreds of angry, racist white parents, I did not permit their anger to overwhelm me. Primarily, I wanted to understand it. I was intellectually curious and moved toward them with interest in both their anger and their larger experience. Other people might have been afraid when confronted with the parents' anger, or they may have been angry with them. That was the concern of the two board members who attended one of the first meetings.

Of course, the white parents' angry, racist expressions affected me. The impulse that arose within me was disgust, and I wanted to distance from them. However, group members reveled in the fact that the others felt and behaved the same as they did. They were far from disgusted with one another. Their thinking labeled their racist beliefs and feelings as justified and appropriate, but their feelings were in charge of their thinking.

I was acting from my solid self while relating to them. I had thought through certain principled beliefs about relating to them. I was anxious, but I was able to override my anxiety and stay faithful to my principles and beliefs. The crowd was not acting from their solid selves. They strongly fused with one another, trading pseudo selves, emboldening one another like mobs do, shouting out, "That's right!" Initially, very few people were making use of their intellect except to rationalize their emotionality. They were automatically reacting to their sense of threat.

Over time, while working with these people, I saw some of them build a bit more of solid self. I saw them reacting less with feeling, and, instead, thinking more about what had been going on. This increased level of thinking was critical for the positive direction that developed later in the group life. As Bowen suggested, they felt less like victims and began to take thoughtful responsibility for their own lives and goals.

A well-differentiated person is not cold, distant, rigid, and unfeeling. Lower-level people often believe that the free, unfettered expression of feelings represents a high level of functioning and using the intellect is a defense against it. If I had said something to the parents along the lines of, "Let's all calm down and think about what is going on here." I would have been booed out of the room. Their feelings were guiding them at this time and a simple injunction to be more thoughtful was not going to change that. I had to relate to the feelings without focusing on them or using them for my own purposes the way demagogic leaders would do.

Repeatedly, Bowen (1978) emphasizes that when he refers to higher-level people, he does not mean that differentiation is an anti-feeling concept. For example, he says:

> They [higher-level people] are able to live more freely and to have more satisfying emotional lives within the emotional system. They can participate fully in emotional events knowing they can extricate themselves with logical reasoning when the need arises (369);

and

> . . . the marriage is a functioning partnership. The spouses can enjoy the full range of emotional intimacy without either being "de-selfed" by the other. They can be autonomous selfs either together or alone (370).

Those people who are more fused are easily flooded by their own emotionality and that of others. Their feelings are their guides in life; they act based on what "feels right." They think that if they "feel it," it must be a fact. They have not thought through a consistent set of beliefs and principles by which they guide themselves through the challenges of life, nor have they thought about how they will function in their relationships with others. The basis of their decisions will vary from moment to moment and circumstance to circumstance. Feeling-based impulses will be in charge of making major life decisions. The aim of such action is to reduce anxiety. Somehow, I understood this about the parents.

People in polarized positions often appear to have strongly held, principled positions (whether on the left or the right politically). However, they reveal their emotionality in their inability to tolerate those on the other side. There is rigidity to their beliefs and they cannot listen to or think along with others. This is evidence of their fusion in the system. They are less likely to recognize all of the relevant facts and they are highly selective about what they consider factual. Any facts that do not fit their beliefs will be ignored, discarded as irrelevant, or rejected as lies. Usually their beliefs lack consistency along a range of issues.

Well-differentiated people are not intellectually rigid. They are comfortable with changing their minds if new information warrants it and deciding an earlier position of theirs was wrong. They will not change their minds because of group coercion or threats. They do not get anxious and give in if a friend threatens them with rejection because of their beliefs. A fear of being alone does not cause them to conform in order to be accepted. None of my friends rejected me because of my actions with the white parents' group, but they definitely disapproved and distanced themselves from my actions.

Well-differentiated people act on their thought-through convictions and beliefs. They are less hypocritical, saying one thing and doing another. They are less focused on their "rights" and what they think is due them (for example, respect), and more focused on their own responsible action to achieve what they want out of life. While they may work hard for what they believe in, their goals do not usually include the other-focused stance of "defeating the enemy."

Lower-level people may be highly intelligent. They may be able to use their intellect to support their emotionally-based decisions and arguments, so they often have elaborate rationales for their beliefs. However, they are less able to view facts in an objective way and to assess the reality of what is going on around them, especially in their relationships. If they are in a leadership position, they tend to demand loyalty and obedience and they condemn doubting. They may be dogmatic and dictatorial leaders.

Fusion and differentiation in relationships

For his use of the term "differentiation," Bowen took his lead from cell biology. The fertilized egg starts as a one-celled organism, and then it begins to divide into many cells. As the cells divide, they also begin to differentiate into what will become different parts of the body. These separate, new groupings of cells eventually take on a variety of bodily purposes and become quite unlike each other in both appearance and function, and yet they are all part of the same body. They are still connected and the functioning of one part affects the functioning of other parts. For example, the heart cannot do the job of the lungs and yet their functioning is interconnected.

Differentiation is not about distancing from others. It is not true differentiation if there is no connection to others. Differentiation is about a connection to others that is more effective than the fused togetherness that ignores individuality and confuses responsibility. Among the well-differentiated people in your congregation are those who can best relate to a broad range of people in the church. They are not cliquish or elitist.

"Closeness as sameness" is a very strong theme in many churches. This is the spiritual version of our romantic fantasies. Many people join a church with the hope of finding a kind of harmonious peace. They want that from their pastor's sermons or from fellowship in the church. They do not want to hear about the conflicts of the world. For them, spirituality means escape from all of the stress and struggles of life.

However, the idea of closeness as sameness is the best recipe for creating conflict in the church. Because of the life force of individuality, it is not possible for people to be the same, apart from whether that is desirable or not. With couples, conflict tends to arise when one partner wants the other to be what that partner wants. The same thing happens in a community like the church when we want others to think or believe the way we do.

The more we believe that we all have to think, feel, and act the same, the more difficulties there are in our relationships. This belief is destructive. It is a precondition for polarization. When people begin to argue intensely over whose "sameness" we are going to follow, then we are polarized. The irony is that this happens even in the groups that have separated from other separatist groups. Currently, in the United States, for example, even the deeply conservative members of the Tea Party have difficulty finding commonality with each other. They are torn between those who believe "my approach to these issues is more pure than yours" and those who might take a more moderate stance. This tends to be true of all separatist movements, on the left as well as on the right. On the left, in the sixties, it happened in hippie communes. When one group leaves a church or a denomination over polarized issues, it is not long before those group members are fighting with each other over who is most correct. This is fusion at work.

The group as an emotional unit and relationship focus versus goal focus

As Bowen observed the more troubled families he was working with back in the early fifties, he began thinking of them as being a kind of big emotional mass. In the families with the most difficulties, it seemed to him that if one member had an itch, another member would scratch himself. If he asked a question of one family member, another would answer. One family member could have a serious symptom, and if the therapist helped resolve the symptom in that person, then another person in the family would become symptomatic in some other way as the anxiety shifted in the system. The emotional boundaries between family members were weak and poorly defined, and the symptomatic expression of anxiety in the family could jump around from person to person.

Those family members tended to be highly reactive and sensitive to the feelings and opinions of others. They could not be impartial about those opinions. They were not comfortable with the idea that others might have feelings and opinions different from their own, especially if there were any sense in which the others were critical of self's own positions. This sensitivity and reactivity to others is a key aspect of lower levels of differentiation.

Lower-level people are relationship oriented. They base their feelings on how they think others feel about them. The paradox is that in spite of their strong relationship focus, they tend to have relationships that are more problematic. They want others to feel a certain way. Much of their life energy will focus on relationships rather than moving toward personal life goals. They may do for others as a way to gain love, or directly seek the love and support of others, and they become reactive if they do not get it. They are quick to accuse others of not loving them if those others do not fulfill their hopes or expectations, and they believe they cannot be happy unless the right people love them. They are searching for the ideal relationship as a life goal.

Frequently, because of consistent disappointment in this effort, some people totally withdraw from relationships and become hermit-like. They refuse to seek closeness with others or, if they are in a relationship, they are emotionally unavailable. This does not mean they are without feelings, but just the opposite. The feeling world is too intense for them and they become relationship phobic. They appear to have no feelings, but in actuality it is just the opposite. They are highly relationship focused. They want them but cannot tolerate the feelings involved.

If lower-level people do make plans or set life goals, they fail to stick to them and follow through. This is because of where they think they stand in relationships and the sense of threat they feel. This is a primary issue. "Things" happen that get in the way of fulfilling their goals. Usually these "things" have to do with relationships. Their long terms goals tend to be vague, perhaps along the lines of, "I want to be happy," or "be successful and make money," or "be famous," or even "just be a good Christian." They do not think clearly about what it might require of them to achieve this. Others are rigid in their goals and ignore the impact on others or the damage done to self in pursuing them.

In general, well-differentiated people have a better life course. They have thought through their goals for life, decided on the kind of person they want to be in their relationships with family, friends, their community, and coworkers, and they take responsibility for their choices. They are accountable to others. They will live up to their commitments.

Even these well-differentiated people can move toward the behaviors of the less well-differentiated if there is more anxiety. The more anxiety they experience, they may, like poorly differentiated people, be willing to compromise self's principles or goals in order to regain a sense of stability, or to do whatever is needed to reduce the anxiety. Given enough anxiety, they move in this direction. It is a rare person who has no susceptibility to anxiety. However, if they do move in a negative direction, they are frequently more resilient and able to recover quickly once they understand what is happening. In general, well-differentiated people are more tolerant of their anxiety and do not need to act impulsively to try to reduce it.

Differentiation and polarization

Although I knew nothing about Bowen theory during the ten years I was a parish-based pastor, now, looking back, I can say who the well-differentiated people in my church were and be thankful for their presence. They saved us all a lot of grief and turmoil by their more mature abilities. In any church, they are the people who are not caught up in polarization and who act on behalf of what is good for the church. They are also clear in their own principled beliefs and actions. The church leaders I mention in the sixth chapter are such people.

Well-differentiated people avoid becoming polarized. As Bowen (1978) succinctly puts it:

> A differentiated self is one who can maintain emotional objectivity while in the midst of an emotional system in turmoil [as in polarized debates between others], yet at the same time actively relate to key people in the system (485).

The Greek word for anxiety is related to the word for "narrow." As anxiety increases, it decreases peoples' ability to think clearly about the situation. It interferes with their ability to function effectively within the situation. It tends to intensify the difficulties and send the situation spinning further out of control. It narrows the perceptual focus so that people cannot see all that is going on in a situation, which reduces the options for action.

As the fusion-based push for closeness as sameness becomes more powerful, and as people narrowly focus on this, the likelihood of conflict and polarization grows. As people attempt to subdue the individuality of those who disagree with them, then others do the same with them. When things are calm in the church and the level of anxiety is low, we are more likely to be open and accepting of differences and other peoples' individuality. We even celebrate our differences. In times of intense anxiety, this concept gets lost quickly.

When the anxiety of a community goes up, the fusion forces take over. Certain fusion-based behaviors control the situation.

- We do not listen well or comprehend the concerns of the other;

- We focus on what we think are the problems of others rather than our own;
- We try to change them rather than focus on changing self;
- We are not open about what lies behind our own concerns or those of others;
- We do not think reasonably and objectively;
- We are less flexible and adaptive to the reality of the situation;
- Our egos become involved; and
- We do not explore common ground to determine how we can work together toward a solution to the situation.

This is what happened in the race riot situation.

Polarized people's emotional reactivity and their sensitivity to whether another person is a friend or a foe on the issue that concerns them is evidence of this fusion. Polarizing leaders will pander to the anxiety within people and use it to promote their own agendas. Using triangles is a way of life for them, often gaining unity within their group by focusing on some external enemy and mobilizing against and defeating the enemy. They tell each other stories about the evils of the other side. They are happy when they hear followers repeating their arguments, and they are unhappy whenever anyone in the group tries to think for self or expresses doubts.

The more mature people in the white parents' group were less anxious. These more emotionally mature leaders emerged as the leaders in the group, and, luckily, some of them were elected to leadership positions. They more quickly saw that black people were not really their enemy, and that the educational system was not intentionally oppressing them. They eventually saw that current educational policies were the real threat to their children getting the education and jobs they needed.

These leaders were able to step back from their original anger and the attitudes that they knew were wrong, even though the group never openly discussed it. No one, including me, ever said, "We have to change our racist attitudes." They thought more clearly than the more emotional members with whom they were also good friends. I was very thankful that this group of people existed.

Well-differentiated people are not going to be polarizers. Again, I turn to Bowen (1978) to summarize the point I want to make here.

> Changing self involves finding a way to listen to the attacks of the other without responding, of finding a way to live with what is without trying to change it, of defining one's own beliefs and convictions without attacking those of the other, and in observing the part that self plays in the situation (178).

Defining a self in the anxious situation

Differentiation simply requires someone who is willing to say to self, consciously or unconsciously, "Hey, I am not going to rush to action on this, or just follow the anxious crowd. I want to think through the situation, identify what principles of mine are relevant here, and see what makes sense to me." This stance is not an automatic, "over-againstness," although more-fused people in the community often perceive it this way. They see it as a stubborn, selfish, or disloyal act. Martin Luther was a lowly priest in the church who disagreed with some of its practices. He thought through the theological issues of grace and redemption for himself and eventually declared this thinking in his *Ninety-Five Theses*. It was not his intent to leave or cause a split in the church. He simply wanted a discussion on what made sense theologically.

However, when examined by the church authorities and called upon to recant his beliefs, he said, "Here I stand. I can do no other." This is truly differentiation of self. The more-fused leadership of the church could not tolerate his more-differentiated individuality and he was excommunicated. There is sometimes a price for differentiating a self. Jesus on the cross tells us this as well.

Even though differentiation is the way systems change, the goal is not about trying to change others. It is not even a tricky, reverse psychology attempt to change others, which is the way fusion operates. If the focus is on how to change others, it is not differentiation and it will fail. Differentiation is simply about defining self, articulating what makes sense to self after thinking through the issues in a particular conflict or situation, and determining what self will and will not do in response to those particular circumstances. It is about a different way of relating to others that, over time, can improve the connection with others. The paradox is that differentiation of self is the way that leads to growth and change in a congregation or any other kind of emotional system.

Objectivity and seeing the bigger picture

The challenge for anyone wanting to help an unhealthy system function more effectively is to see the big picture. Too often, we narrowly (from anxiety) focus on a single problem, like white racism. We think, "That is the problem." We ignore everything else that provides a larger context for the problem and how the problem is only a piece of a larger issue; it is only a piece of a larger pie. The problem is in the whole pie, not just the one piece. In this circumstance, a focus on trying to fix the problem only makes things worse. The liberal teachers in the high school focused on the white kids as the problem and things got worse. They did not have the objectivity to see the part they themselves played in the circumstances leading to the riot.

We are highly subjective creatures. This means we are the subject of our experience. Quite naturally, we see almost everything that happens in our lives from our own specific point of view. We focus on how people and events affect us. It is very difficult to see our part in the reactions of others, or how we affect them. In counseling, I sometimes ask a spouse, "What do you think your partner is up against in living with you?" Frequently, this is such a new thought that they are surprised to consider it. It is so very difficult to step outside of ourselves and be more objective, but it is not impossible. Having enough objectivity to see all of the functional parts of an emotional system, and especially the part that self plays in it, is critical to being a better leader.

Marital counselors can get themselves into an awkward position with a couple if they decide that one partner has a particular problem that needs to be fixed, as obvious as that problem might seem. If the counselor decides that the problem is a husband's chauvinism, for example, and joins a triangle with the wife to try to fix him, it is likely that things will become more polarized between the husband and wife. The counselor will not be helpful. The husband's chauvinism does not even have to be labeled as such for the marital situation to worsen.

I brought a certain amount of typical male chauvinism into my relationship with Lois when we married in 1967. Normally, rather than react to it and try to fight me, she would just more clearly define herself to me regarding what she would and would not do. I do not think she ever once directly accused me of being a chauvinist even though, as an early supporter of NOW (National Organization of Women), she certainly knew what it was. Her behavior put the ball in my court. I had to rethink my attitudes if I wanted to stay married to her (as I did). Her intent was not to change me but to define herself to me. This self-definition challenged me to think through my own beliefs and behaviors.

We are getting to the heart of Bowen theory when we can see self's own functioning and remain in control of it in the midst of a highly anxious situation. In working with the white parents, I was constantly watching myself in order not to come off with any typical attitudes toward them. As I said in the first chapter, my different way of being with them was clearly noticed, which was illustrated colorfully when the president of the white parents' group bluntly asked me why I was doing what I was doing when the church had not treated them well. He recognized that I was not behaving like the typical pastor who might set out to condemn their racism.

Conclusion

I want to give you a guarantee. The better differentiation of self there is among the members of your congregation (especially its leaders) the better your congregation will be able to deal with the challenges it faces in accomplishing its mission in the world and in regulating its own communal life. The good news is that by dint of hard work, we can all improve our functional level of differentiation.

I frequently use a quote from Michael Kerr (1988), who succeeded Bowen at the Georgetown Family Center in Washington, DC, which I have adapted to use for the church. He was talking about families, but his words easily apply to the church. Here is my modified version of what he said:

> The higher the level of differentiation of people in a family [church, synagogue, or faith group], the more they can cooperate, look out for one another's welfare, and stay in adequate emotional contact during stressful as well as calm periods. The lower the level of differentiation, the more likely the family [faith group], when stressed, will regress to selfish, aggressive, and avoidance behaviors; cohesiveness, altruism, and cooperativeness will break down." (93)

Differentiating a self takes courage. It takes a willingness to stand alone. This was true when I lacked the support of my colleagues and friends while working with the white parents' group. If I had thought that I needed their support to continue in the work, and that they were wrong for not supporting me, it would have been game over. Of course, they, more than a year later, came around and congratulated me, but I did not need this praise from them to have the sense that something important was going on. I was happy that they finally understood what I was doing—they got it—but that was not critical for me.

5

Emotional Process in Society and Polarization

The eighth concept of emotional process in society

Dr. Bowen formalized the societal emotional process as the eighth concept in his theory in 1975. Initially, he called the concept "societal regression." He recognized that, "A nation can go into regression, just as a family does, and a nation can pull out in predictable ways" (Kerr and Bowen, 384). Even though he did not get further than "a beginning theory about society as an emotional system" (386), Bowen gave us a framework for understanding human functioning at the social level beyond the family. The whole of his theory applies (with the necessary changes) at a societal level and it accounts for how society progresses and functions more effectively, as well as how it regresses to less effective functioning. His theory illuminates what happened in the critical incident of the race riot I described in the first chapter—the sources of chronic anxiety feeding it and how things developed afterwards through my work with the white parents' group.

Of the four basic mechanisms for managing anxiety within the nuclear family emotional system (compliance, marital conflict, projection to a child, emotional distancing) projection and distancing also apply to how a society deals with anxiety. In the family, these mechanisms emerge as the level of anxiety increases in response to some sort of stress. As the chronic anxiety continues, the use of these mechanisms leads to the emergence of symptoms. The focus is on these symptoms as the problem with an individual in the family (the individual model) or in the relationship (dyadic model). While family systems theory looks at these symptoms in the context of the family and its emotional process, we see a parallel when the anxiety in a society leads to conflict.

For example, the mechanism of projection is a popular way of dealing with problems at a societal level. We have sometimes called it scapegoating. By the 1960s, when there were interracial conflicts, many white people might have thought (even if they did not say it aloud) that "the problem" was "uppity black people." They would say, "If they would just calm down, everything will be okay." "They" were the problem. If black people calmed down, and "stayed in their place," then white society could also calm down and all would be right in the world. White people did not see their part in the problems. They projected their anxiety onto black people.

A certain number of people, mostly liberals like me, thought that racist white people were the problem. The same projection process had taken on a new focus. This focus included making a joke of characters like Archie Bunker and his attitudes. We focused on helping black people reduce the social injustice they experienced, but we were blaming the white people, and their "system" for holding them back. Thus, the liberal teachers, as well as the administration at the high school, had been telling the white kids that they were the problem, and their resentment led them to react just like acting-out adolescents in a family.

Do not get me wrong here. There is no question about the reality of racism. Also as a liberal, I believe government can have a helpful role in dealing with the problems in society. I support the civil rights laws, along with the whole range of related government interventions. However, just like any other group in society, liberals can be too simplistic in their understanding of social problems and what is required to fix them. The same emotional processes that lead to societal regression can govern them.

The concepts of family systems theory also apply to the functioning of sub-groups within society, such as the workplace, the church, a social club, a neighborhood, a school, or whatever. Using the concept of differentiation of self, Bowen accounted for variations in how some families and social groups functioned more or less effectively than others. This variability in functioning helped explain how a society could degenerate from or progress toward more effective functioning.

Bowen's concept of emotional distancing, or cutoff, is especially relevant to the level of chronic social anxiety. As society becomes more scattered, with adult children moving far away from their parents and often having little significant emotional contact, the amount of inter-generational cutoff tends to grow. In addition, as more immigrants come into a new country and are cut off from their families by more than geographical distance, these adults might have higher levels of unresolved emotional attachment to their families and across multiple generations. As a result, the emotional process within society heats up even more. Cutoff happens between people and their institutions as well. The white parents were emotionally cut off from their church, even though they still attended. I will explore the relevance of the concept of emotional cutoff more in the eighth chapter.

Factors affecting chronic anxiety in society

Polarization is a symptom, not a cause. Symptoms develop over time in response to the buildup of chronic anxiety. Symptoms let us know that there is a problem that is not being addressed, but the symptoms are not the problem. The emotional issues leading to the riot were the symptom.

Bowen (1978) asserted that there are critical issues that raise the level of chronic anxiety in society. They are the obvious, emotionally-laden, sociopolitical, polarized issues that demand our attention and that the media highlight. Among these are the population explosion, the diminishing amount of raw materials that are critical to survival (good air, water, and an adequate food supply being central ones), and the pollution of the earth that also contributes to this diminishment. These are "slowly threatening the balance of life necessary for human survival" (386). These facts are the driving force behind today's chronic anxiety and that which lies behind many people's sense of immediate threat.

Like all instinctive creatures, we want to maintain the basic necessities of life that keep us alive. Food, water, air, and physical well-being are, of course, some of these necessities. Others include a stable family that provides adequate shelter, reproductive opportunities, and a safe environment in which to raise children. Safeguarding the earth and protecting its ability to produce food is critical. Historically, competing for control of these essentials caused most of the world's conflicts in previous centuries. When these essentials are endangered, the level of chronic anxiety in a society increases and the society is more reactive.

Such increasing levels of chronic anxiety are often beyond our immediate awareness. On the one hand, we are aware of issues like overcrowding, but not of the toll that it is taking on us physically as well as emotionally. On the other hand, we may not be consciously aware of the buildup of toxins in our air and water, or of decreased nutrients in our food, in spite of how these things present physical challenges to our bodies that show up long after damage has occurred. Our bodies are suffering the consequences of this reality, and this affects our level of chronic anxiety, even when we are not aware of it.

The world's population grew by a billion people in just the twelve years between 1999 and 2011. In October of 2011, earlier than expected, the world population hit 7 billion, and the United Nations warned that the world population could more than double by the end of the century. If the entire world consumed resources at the level of North America, the earth could only sustain around two billion people.

In agrarian societies, where people have maintained their connection with the land and its produce, these issues are generally more clearly in their consciousness. Farmers, for example, are some the most environmentally aware people on earth. Whole societies have died out when there is famine or drought, when the land has lost its ability to sustain crop growth. With the increasing difficulty of feeding people, the population of the world is hurtling toward an unsustainable level, adding to problems with the environment and the earth's diminishing resources.

In the modern, urban world that is based on a market economy, people tend to take for granted the land's ability to produce adequate food and water for the world's population. In addition, they have little awareness of the toll exerted on them by a polluted environment. There is little direct awareness of the underlying agrarian issues for a reasonable population size. It is easy to lose touch with these underlying issues, even though they may be exacting a toll on the population.

Monetary issues (like fewer well-paying jobs) have contributed to the level of acute anxiety in society, which over time, added to the level of chronic anxiety. In December of 2011, the United States Census Bureau announced that 48 percent of Americans live at poverty or low-income levels (defined as an annual income of $47,000 for a family of four). The bureau said the inflation-adjusted average earnings for the bottom 20 percent of families (earning under $15,000) have been falling since 1979. The next 20 percent (earning up to $37,000) have remained flat over that period. The top 5 percent of the population has seen their earnings grow by 64 percent to over $313,000 annually. The numbers of those who are defined as "middle-class" are steadily shrinking. The increasing polarization of society has been growing over the same period.

Our market economy is hugely complicated, and there are no easy answers to the complex economic issues we face. There are so many interrelated issues that intervention at one level can create unexpected, negative results at another level. Today, anyone who is feeling the economic pinch is likely experiencing a higher level of anxiety. As increasing numbers of families have this experience, almost automatically, more groups emerge with rhetoric that ignites discord and conflict.

When we add other specific issues (for example, government debt, an inadequate tax base to support government services, the possible collapse of the financial system, the lack of good health services, the decreasing ability of people to get a mortgage and buy a house, and the increasing shipment of jobs overseas), we can see how all of these factors contribute to a surge in chronic anxiety. The general sense of threat in society increases and people become more reactive and polarized.

People's need for an adequate income critically affects their levels of anxiety; consequently, having a well-paying job helps alleviate that anxiety. If people have enough income and feel physically safe, they tend to be happier and less anxious. Issues like the loss of an adequate income and the level of safety are immediate, acute stressors affecting the quality of life and the level of anxiety. High levels of unemployment result in higher levels of societal anxiety.

If people do have jobs, often they are paid at a lower level than they had been paid previously. It is a situation of crowding (too many people) on the one hand and scarcity on the other (too few resources). People have material expectations for how they ought to be able to live, and they can see no hope of achieving it. Through the triangular mechanisms, there are many scapegoats available for people to blame, saying, "This is why we are in trouble." This projection process is the customary way people attempt to deal with their growing sense of insecurity.

These issues clarify the situation leading up to the race riot in my city. As in most industrialized cities at that time, there were a decreasing number of jobs available. Those that had been available to the blue-collar, white community, were increasingly going to black people. As the white parents retired, they did not see their own sons and daughters taking their jobs. Through a powerful community organization, black groups had been able to get large corporations in the city to commit a number of jobs to them. The anxiety among the white population related to the reduction of a critical resource (jobs and income) complicated by their existing racist attitudes, both of which were important factors leading to the riot. The diminishing number of jobs was a critical issue for the moment; racial attitudes had existed for a long time. Tension increased between the two races around the availability of jobs. To put it in the terms Bowen used, there were too many people for the diminished number of jobs—with a kind of population explosion as the black community increasingly took jobs that the white population had previously seen as theirs.

In the course of working with them, the white parents' group increasingly understood that these economic issues were central to the community and that they were more important than their attitudes toward black people. This clarity is part of what helped to ameliorate the racial attitudes and allowed them to begin to work with each other rather than fight with each other. With regard to the school system, job skills and training became the primary focus. The emotional shock wave of decreasing employment opportunities for an increasingly large working population brought about the immediate circumstance that triggered the riot.

The polarizing process

The polarizing process is one of the automatic social mechanisms people develop when there is chronic anxiety. The two sides of an issue divide into opposing camps with a significant amount of distance between them so they are unable to maintain a viable emotional connection. It is like a marital conflict where the partners describe themselves as "poles apart" when they come into my office for counseling. In marital conflict, as their anxiety increases, the partners take on increasingly radical stands, hold to them dogmatically, and their fights escalate, with each partner reacting more to the other's reaction.

Neither side is willing to adapt or give in to the other, nor can they figure out a way to co-exist, or find common ground, or cooperate. They often vilify each other. The intensity of polarized conflict is so high that they spend a large part of their lives being preoccupied with the conflict and with developing arguments and battle strategies to defeat the others. It becomes an all-consuming passion. Each self is focused on the other. They are not working at better defining their own self. It is the same in the larger society.

In terms of marriage difficulty, there are many issues that two married people can fight over. Many marital counselors mistakenly focus on these issues and get involved in the content of their fights. Their belief is that the couple needs to learn how to communicate better, to be more caring for each other, and learn how to negotiate their differences more effectively. My own stance is, "These are two otherwise smart, and even caring, people. They do not need me to jump in and take a side on who is right or wrong or to tell them how they can resolve their problems by teaching them communication strategies."

They need help to see how the underlying anxiety is affecting them, as well as help to move to a more thoughtful place where they can figure out these difficulties for themselves. Getting to this ideal outcome is always a challenge because of the significant amount of emotionality involved. Bowen theory helps to explain how the process works, and what I, as a marriage counselor, can do for my part in the process. That is what I am trying to explore in this book as we tackle the parallel issue of polarizing emotional process for the church in society.

In our divided world today, this social-emotional process of polarization is equally true of both liberal and conservative sides. Emotional process is not about one's political stance or commitments. Both sides are able to function, but, in the extreme phase, the two sides are totally repellent to each other. They reject almost everything the other says or does. If there is some apparent agreement, they think suspiciously, "they are up to something." Neither side gives in to the other side. Compromise is a dirty word. They concede no territory. It is difficult to bring about any mutual or joint decisions with regard to a truce because there remains a belief that the other side will get the advantage. There is little interest in talking or communicating with the other side—"I have nothing to say to them." If I had proposed joint white and black parents' groups too early in the process, I would have been kicked out of the group.

Approaches that focus on getting opposing sides to communicate usually fail at this level of intensity. If they do have meetings for each side to talk to the other, it is frequently a disaster. The intensity only increases. Each side is determined to show how the other side just does not get it. It does not take long for them to be shouting at one another. There are rigid defensive maneuvers, as when the parents in the riot case counseled their children not to take any abusive behavior from the other side. If necessary, they strike out violently to protect their dignity. The issues involved consume the thinking and energy of the combatants.

There is lack of recognition that the two sides are hugely invested in each other—this is the fusion. Everything they do anticipates what the other may say or do. They are always thinking in defensive and offensive ways. Winning the battle is the issue. It can escalate to outright, violent warfare. They even use the language of war and violence in their rhetoric. Some combatants may begin to suffer physical or emotional difficulties related to the stress of the situation and the impact of their anxiety.

In terms of the social triangles, there will be apparent partisans who take advantage of the situation to promote themselves and their self-interests. Some of these will be politicians. High anxiety situations present a good opportunity to develop demagogic positions and a sense of importance. They will come forward to exercise leadership for the group against the perceived opponents, or the enemy, and then profit from it in some way.

There is a kind of tribal warfare between the polarized groups. Tribalism is pandemic in most of the world conflicts today, as in the Middle East. Peoples' loyalty or commitment is more to the group, or the tribe (the political party), than it is to a nation or a government of laws. Winning honor and recognition for "our side," and retribution for any shaming or dishonor done to us by the other side are the primary goals of the tribe.

The primary issue, though, is the higher level of anxiety and the corresponding lack of functional differentiation. Chronic anxiety and the functional level of differentiation correlate in reverse. The more there is of one, generally, then the less there is of the other. Down through the ages, people have had disagreements over the kind of issues on which we take polarized stances today. There is little that is new in the issues themselves. The difference today is the much higher level of anxiety.

In societies where there is a higher than average level of differentiation and, as a result, less chronic anxiety, they manage to live peaceably together without the open warfare of polarization. They are friendly and caring toward one another, and they welcome each other into their houses for meals together. There is a more civil atmosphere. They do not have the idea that their differences have to be resolved before they can be friends. They know if there is any chance of resolving the issues, polarized fighting over them will only increase the likelihood of failure.

With a lower level of functional differentiation (and consequently higher anxiety), comes a higher level of emotionality. When people are emotionally reactive to one another, there is a heightened sense of the importance of their differences. They cannot hear each other, and they are unwilling to do so. They may even declare that they are "willing to be tolerant to differences, but on this topic? No way!" At extreme levels of the conflict, people even go around the country, looking for those who disagree with them and try to find ways to shut down their point of view. Programs like the Spanish Inquisition come to mind. This occurred when the society and the church were extremely anxious and focused on the purity of belief as a solution to their increased anxiety.

The polarizing process is a natural phenomenon in society as a way to deal with higher levels of anxiety. As a solution, polarization is useless for dealing with the underlying issues, but it helps the contenders feel somewhat better about themselves by allowing them to blame others for their problems without worrying about their own adequacy (or lack thereof).

Moving toward a positive direction

The most effective approach to this buildup of anxiety and triangulation is differentiation of self (as described in chapter four) and, as a result, people taking more responsibility for self. This interrupts the emotional process. It inhibits the other-focus and brings the focus back to self and how self is functioning in relation to others, what self is contributing to the problem, and how self is going to be responsible for changing and behaving differently. The regressive social process will continue until one or more people make this kind of change. If most of the group goes in this direction, as with the white parents' group, they will make progress that is more effective.

Without knowing anything about the Bowen concepts, this is how I functioned in response to race riot at the school. I did not connect with the white parents in order to change them. I thought that was their job. I thought my job was trying to maintain an emotional connection with them, to understand them better and to do what I could to be a resource to them. Only in vague terms did I think of myself as a resource, helping them to move from a "more feeling" orientation to a "more thinking" orientation, but this is what happened.

A society is not a thing. It is not independent of the people in it. Society is the sum total of the families that exist within it and the emotional processes they employ. As a conglomerate, it may be possible to say that with a higher level of differentiation of a group of families, then the sum total of that group could represent a well-differentiated society, and vice versa. I have no idea of the basic level of differentiation of the white parents' group, but I believe that their functional level of differentiation improved significantly from the time I started working with them. The shift from feeling to thinking demonstrates this.

Families and society have a reciprocal relationship with one another. Parents transmit certain cultural and social beliefs to their children from the social environment. Each family has a somewhat different take on their economic/social/political beliefs (like racist views toward black people), and they each communicate these various beliefs to the children. Families may share many of the same views, or they may diverge. As individual families develop their views, they also begin to shape the views of society in which they live. The emotional processes involved in both the family and the society are mutually interrelated.

Addressing emotional reactivity (without adding to it) early in the process makes it more manageable—like my being on the spot at the time of the riot. Leaders who are aware of emotional processes may be able to see the buildup of anxiety in a group (like a congregation) and interrupt it before it is expressed in symptomatic ways. If the liberal, white teachers at the high school were aware of what was happening in the lead-up to the riot, that tensions were increasing, they were likely being more reactive to it themselves. They did not see how they were a part of the emotional process and how they contributed to the tension. They could not get outside of the emotional process. They continued to contribute to it after the riot by reacting to the formation of the white parents' group. They advised the school board not to cooperate with the group, and they let me know what they thought of me.

Politics, politicians, the church, and polarization

The political arena is a perfect place to play out polarized stances. Politicians, whose primary goal is to get elected or re-elected, can capitalize on the chronic anxiety in society and make use of the acute situations that develop to win votes.

Politicians who participate in this process become functionally fused to the anxiety of those in their constituency and the popular mood of the times. They are often willing to abandon their own professed principles for the sake of winning votes, and they do it under the guise of being "principled." They make an emotionally-based decision in order to avoid the anxiety of losing an election. Their narrow self-interest takes precedence over the larger interests of the society.

Politicians need two things to win: votes and money. These are their springboards to power. If they can bring the two together, they usually win. It is notoriously difficult to know what a politician actually believes. They "perform" in an effort to win over their power base. They typically say whatever the voters— and those with the money—want to hear. Any politician who goes against the opinions of the anxious voters, or offends those with money, usually loses.

This view of politicians should not make us cynical about politics. It is easy to go in that direction. If a large enough group of people can become less anxious and more thoughtful, and be willing to make tough decisions and stand behind them with their votes, then society can head in a new direction. When that group of people begins to make their voices heard, the political leaders will emerge to carry out the mandate. A more thoughtful and less reactive electorate will give us those kinds of politicians. Again, this is not about a particular political persuasion, left or right, but about the way the process works.

Occasionally, a politician comes along who presents a more solid self and says what he or she really believes. If these beliefs are focused on where he or she wants to head in society, and not on fighting those on the other side, as in polarization, then a real option is offered to the voter (if the voter agrees with the political philosophy of the politician).

For change to happen, there first has to be some kind of shift in the voters. This is where the church has an impact. Those churches willing to take on the project of becoming better differentiated (that is, less anxious and more thoughtful, and clarifying principles around what is important, as well as being less reactive and less polarized) contribute positively to political discourse. I am not talking about churches taking stands on specific issues, but instead, engendering the kind of atmosphere that encourages decent and thoughtful political discourse to take place.

Conclusion

The Bowen theory's approach to polarization in the church and society provides a way of thinking about what creates the difficulties involved, along with ways of moving beyond them, and it helps us confront the challenges that can block change. It does not offer direct answers or give prescriptions for what to do; each situation is different. However, the principles involved are the same. It involves a process that takes time. In general, quick-change solutions may look effective in the short term but they are also easily short-circuited. Taking the long view, and having an accurate understanding of what is happening, brings about more solid and lasting change.

In the next three chapters, I describe three specific examples from my own life experience of how polarization in social groups was either avoided or reduced and how positive change took place. In these cases, the principles involved, not the specific outcomes, are most important.

6

Avoiding a Potentially Polarizing Situation in a Local Church

The background

After serving about two years at the church in the community where the race riot happened, it was clear to me and to a few other leaders in the church that the future of the congregation was limited. We had a significantly older, mostly retired membership and we were not winning many new members from the new neighborhood residents who were of a different cultural, economic, and religious tradition. The change in the makeup of the community was accelerating due, in part, to the proven practices by the banks and the real estate companies of "redlining" specific neighborhoods. The real estate agents would show houses in our neighborhood only to poorer black people, and the banks would not make loans to white people who wanted to buy there.

In addition, I would occasionally make the observation to my session (the board of a Presbyterian church) that it was too bad that our entire budget virtually went into supporting our huge, brick building, and paying staff salaries. We had very little left over for mission efforts, either local or foreign. They shared my concern. I speculated that without some kind of significant change we had maybe five or ten years at the most before we would have to close our doors. These discussions occasionally led to informal brainstorming that went nowhere. We were not seeing answers. Our closest suburban Presbyterian church (only four miles away) had benefited from our loss of membership, and eventually closing the church appeared to be inevitable, but it did not fit with the goals the rest of us had for our church in this community.

There were three other churches (Baptist, Methodist, and Episcopal) in our immediate neighborhood, each facing the same dilemma. My discussions with the pastors at these churches proved they were uninterested in any discussion of the bigger issue or about how we might cooperate more. They each said things did not look so bad to them, even though they admitted exactly the same dynamics were at work. The pastors at these churches were older, and I thought (perhaps cynically), they were just trying to get their church to limp along until they retired.

I was also going through some personal changes at the time in terms of my own career. I had decided to pursue a Doctor of Ministry degree in pastoral counseling and had received the support of my church to do so. I told them that at the end of this program, in about three years' time, I would likely be leaving the church and probably moving to a new city. There was general disappointment, but they accepted my decision. In the meantime, I said, I wanted to work with them to enable them and the church to minister effectively in the neighborhood. This very early announcement of my plans did not seem to create any kind of lame duck status for me. They appreciated hearing about my own plans for my future.

At the beginning of my third year, a new pastor came to the Baptist (American Convention) church three blocks down the street from us. I will call him Bill. He was about my age and he and I hit it off. We had similar interests and commitments to the same kind of ministry and similar mission concerns for our neighborhood. His church had approximately the same number of members as ours and a similar kind of history. I was happy to find such a colleague in ministry and we became friends as well. In our regular get-togethers, we quickly began to discuss the future of our two churches.

The process of a church merger

Bill and I knew that there was such a thing as a union church, one which consists of one merged congregation related officially to their two original denominations. Neither of us had ever heard of a Baptist/Presbyterian union church before. Without mentioning this idea to our church boards, we each explored this concept with our judicatory officials to see if they would block us in any way or support our efforts. Both denominational heads thought this would be a great solution to what they knew would be a problem for them in the future. We all agreed that we did not want our churches to become mission churches, supported only by the judicatories.

Bill and I began to discuss how we might proceed. In the past, members and leaders at each church had said negative things about the other church and its beliefs and practices. Our members (and theirs) had seen the other church as quite different. If I happened to mention something about the Baptists down the street, I would detect a slight sign of disdain on the faces of my members. Bill reported similar kinds of responses in his congregation about "those Presbyterians up the street." The churches had been quite competitive for new members in the past, which had not engendered good feelings. Apart from the denominational differences, members in each church knew little of a factual nature about the other.

Bill and I engaged in careful planning around how we might approach the idea of a union church with our congregations and church leaders. We did not want to do anything to jeopardize it as we were beginning to invest some hope in it. Along with our worship committees, he and I planned a few joint worship services as simple ecumenical events. We worshiped in each other's sanctuaries and both congregations enjoyed having a larger group of people with better singing.

Building on this positive response, we decided to mention it to our boards in a low-key way, without saying it was *the* solution or that we had committed to it, but simply telling them about union churches and how they work. We did not openly express enthusiasm or energy for the idea. We both said that it might not work and that there could be many problems with the idea. We said that, at best, a merger would only have a temporary benefit. We carefully avoided sending the impression that Bill and I were intent on forcing it on our members. In fact, I was quite fine with whatever decision my congregation eventually made. I think I was both genuinely neutral in terms of the decision belonging to the congregation but also hopeful in terms of how I thought it could work. Bill and I both knew that once we had mentioned it to the boards, they would begin to test the response from other church members.

There was a mixed response in both churches. Apparently, there had been a past problem related to competing fall fairs, which used to be very popular in both churches. Nobody could remember specifically what the problem was, and it seemed the original players were long gone. A few people said they would have trouble being part of the same church, theologically, as "those" Baptists or "those" Presbyterians. Bill and I had our own concerns about the differing polities and the theological and sacramental issues involved.

Once the idea had floated through the grapevines of the two churches and our boards got a sense of what members thought, we proposed to each board that the various similar committees of the two churches could have meetings with each other. They could discuss their programs and worship practices. Bill and I chose not to be involved in these meetings, leaving the discussions entirely up to the members involved. Primarily, we did not want to be in the position of pushing solutions to any problems that emerged. Feedback on these meetings was quite positive.

After a few months of this sort of slow process, both boards decided to establish an exploratory committee composed of equal numbers from both churches; the purpose of this committee was to study the question of creating a union church (again, a single congregation related to two denominations) and to determine the practical issues that needed to be addressed. We would have to create entirely new formats for governing our communal life, conducting worship services, and handling sacraments like baptism, as well as managing the theological differences and our relationships to our denominations.

Both boards agreed that forming a union church would mean that one of us would have to sell our church building, and the new congregation would worship in the other one. Everyone saw this, in theory, as a major plus for the plan because this freed up more money for local mission in our neighborhood. No serious discussion had taken place about which church building would be sold, and no one was taking a hard position about it.

The exploratory committee hired two different engineering firms to do a complete examination of each building and to make a report to the committee on the pluses and minuses of each. Both companies went over the buildings in fine detail and gave specific feedback, with dollar amounts, as to which building would be the costliest to repair and maintain. Both companies agreed that the Presbyterian building was in better overall shape and would be the cheapest to maintain on an ongoing basis. We had some small business owners from both churches on the exploratory committee, and because they understood issues regarding capital expenses, they were able to avoid being caught up in sentimental issues and to stay focused on facts. The committee was in agreement with the engineering reports. The Baptist congregation already knew that their building had a number of major problems.

The exploratory committee met with both church boards to present their findings and to create a general plan for how we might proceed toward a merger. Bill and I kept our distance from this process and only responded to questions directed specifically to us. We did not, for example, preach sermons on what a great idea it was to form a union church. When the committee presented their report to each congregation for discussion, the response was positive and members were impressed with the thoroughness of the planning.

We began having more joint Sunday worship services, with Bill and me as worship leaders, functioning as co-pastors. One Sunday, Bill and I did a dialogue sermon in which we openly expressed our apprehensions about the merger and discussed the differing polities and theology of our denominations. We also expressed some ideas about how we thought it could work and said, essentially, we liked what the committee was doing and could work with the proposal.

The outcome and the importance of a principled position

After about a year and a half of planning and discussion, the two congregations voted to form a union church. We also approved a new name and logo for the church. Things moved rapidly after that. The Baptist congregation approved the sale of their building, and everything went incredibly well.

We officially merged the two congregations at a Sunday worship service that began with the Baptists saying "Goodbye" to their building and desanctifying it. We Presbyterians also went through a process of saying goodbye to the church that we had known for many years and looking forward to a "new creation." Then the Baptists marched three blocks to the Presbyterian church, where our congregation welcomed them, joined arms with them, and walked into the sanctuary together. Our members understood that they would have to shift from the pews they had come to consider their own in the sanctuary; we had talked previously about how this repositioning would be a physical symbol of our new life together. We both had excellent turnouts for this event and it was a truly joyous occasion.

Judicatory officials were also a part of the service. They recognized our union and affirmed that, in accord with the

Wednesday, October 28, 2015

And he saith unto them, Whose is this image and superscription? They say unto him, Caesar's. Then saith he unto them, Render therefore unto Caesar the things which are Caesar's; and unto God the things that are God's. ¶ MATTHEW 22 : 20–21

actions of the two denominational bodies, both Bill and I, along with the members and lay leaders, would be welcomed as full ministers, leaders, and members of each other's denominations, with full voting rights and privileges. At the end of the service, we went back outside the sanctuary to release helium-filled balloons. Everyone, adults and children, had written their own prayers for this merger on a small card, along with whatever dedication they made personally to God around it. We attached them to the balloons and then we watched hundreds of them lift into the sky. It was an emotionally moving day for all of us.

Here is what still amazes me about this experience. Because of this merger, we lost only one family. They were an older Baptist couple whose parents had given the money for the stained glass window in their sanctuary, and they said, "It just would not be the same" for them. They had previously moved to the suburbs and decided to join a Baptist church there. They made this move without hostility, saying the merger was a good idea.

Our members displayed a great deal of emotional maturity and sensitivity to potentially difficult issues throughout the process. I had worked with our various committees, and in particular, with the women's association which had strongly affirmed this action. We worked hard on giving up the idea that this was "our" building. Everyone did a fantastic job of recognizing our new model and showed great flexibility around establishing new regimens and new hierarchies. I never once heard anyone say, "But this is how we have always done it." There were small issues that developed over the next year, but there was a good spirit around resolving them and very little reactivity to the changes emerged.

Here is another amazing thing. Bill and I had shared our thinking, early on, that this would give the churches perhaps, at best, another ten to fifteen years of ministry in that community. We did not think of the merger as an ultimate solution given that the community dynamics were not likely to change. The merger happened in early 1975. In fact, that union church still exists today and it is still serving that community. It did, indeed, win new community members to its membership. Today, the neighborhood itself is more beat up than ever. The union church is now an inner-city church, but it has had a strong ministry in that neighborhood and it has a great deal of respect from the community. The other denominational churches, whose pastors did not want to talk with me, have closed their doors.

The church merger process illustrates important aspects of Bowen theory. From what I have already described, many of these will be obvious, but the central one is the importance of maintaining a principled position. Bowen said that differentiation requires thinking through and arriving at one's own principles for living and acting. The major principle that guided us through this merger process was that we all wanted to do a better job of serving the changing community rather than abandoning it. My church had been clear about this from the time that they called me. This was a bigger issue than the importance of the two churches having differing polities and traditions. Throughout the process, anxiety remained at relatively low levels. We achieved a new form of togetherness never before imagined, and we maintained respect for individuality at both the denominational and personal levels.

The qualities of differentiated leadership in this situation

This story represents how well things can go with well-differentiated leadership. I will only address the Presbyterian side of the story, but the Baptists had their own mature leaders. I first want to credit my clerk of session (like the chair of a board) who was extraordinary. She had been a homemaker all her life and had no professional training. But she was well connected to the membership of the church, and she was unflappable. She was a widow, and she was not the usual sort of overfunctioning church leader. She had a life apart from her life in the church. She did not try to make the church into her family.

She could listen to what people said without being reactive or defensive. She could think things through. She had her own sense of personal authority and was fully in charge of herself. She was particularly good at relating to the president of the women's association who could be more reactive. If she had a problem with me, she was not reluctant to say it directly to me. She did not hesitate to be open with me and to report whatever she was hearing. She was specific with names, rather than just saying, "People are saying . . . ," and I never had the sense that she was couching her own positions (in triangular fashion—a concept that I did not know at the time) in the words of other people. This helped me to move toward anyone in the congregation that needed some attention from me. She was quite willing to speak for herself and own her positions whenever I asked, "What do you think?"

This woman modeled a style of leadership for other officers in the church and her relative calmness filtered down into the congregation. She is dead now but I want to honor her by using her real name. I question whether the merger would have happened without Edna. Like me, she did not push the merger as a solution. While it seemed to make sense to her personally, she held her position lightly from the beginning. Like me, she was quite open to whatever the congregation decided. Looking back from my present perspective, it is clear to me that Edna brought to her leadership position relatively little in the way of unresolved emotional attachment. She is probably one of the better differentiated people I have ever known.

Clergy come and go in churches, but the membership stays on. They are the ones who have to live with their decisions, and big decisions like this should be their responsibility. Of course, I had an opinion about what would be good for the church, but I kept that mostly to myself until things had moved quite far into the process. Mostly, when asked, I addressed the practical questions of whether and how a union church would work, but I always said, in conclusion, "You know this is your church and you have to be the ones to decide on its future. It is not my responsibility. As you know, I will not always be here."

The "vision" thing

Too many clergy and church leaders take on agendas for their churches that they want their church to adopt. This happens on small things, as well as major things like this church merger. Such leaders tend to couch their agendas in words like "vision."

When we clergy, or any other leaders, say something like "My vision for this church is . . .", we are operating from an other-focus and not a self-defining-focus. The other-focus is a fused way of functioning. It is a way of saying, "If you do this thing that I think you should do, then I (and maybe you) will feel better. You will be more like I want you to be and that will make me less anxious. I will feel like I have really accomplished something for God." Leaders may deal with their own anxiety by trying to get others to do what they want.

Not all members in a church welcome the message that they are responsible for its future. This is one way I differentiated a self within this congregation. There were several people in my congregation who thought I should tell them what to do about the church's future. They wanted me to lead them. They wanted to know my vision for the church. They said it was my job. When I said the future of the church was not my issue, that it was theirs, they did not like it. A couple of people felt hurt and disappointed in me. They said I was abandoning them. I listened to them and said I understood what they wanted, but it did not make sense to me. I think Edna helped them think this through, and later they said to me, "You were right not to tell us what to do. I feel good about the decision we have made. This really feels like our church."

I did believe that the merger was a good solution, and I may well have communicated that to people through some non-verbal means, but I worked hard to avoid letting my opinions be their guiding principle. I did try to communicate a way of functioning around such challenges. I believed in facing the facts and thinking about ways to deal with the realities these facts presented. I challenged their tendency to coast along and to think that "something will happen," or that I would do something to make things okay. That was not going to happen. They had to take responsibility for their future.

Vision needs to be about self. My vision represents my goals for myself. It is what I will or will not do in particular circumstances as I move toward my goal in life. This is what I am responsible for. I am not responsible for other peoples' vision. Yes, "where there is no vision, the people perish" (*Proverbs* 29:18, KJV), but it is not my job to provide them with a vision. That is a popular misconception about a leader's role. As fusion in action, it would stir up a lot of reactivity in the church. It is a confusion about who is responsible for what. It was simply not my prerogative to decide what this church should do about its future. They developed a vision for their church that was not dependent on me being there or doing it for them.

Some individual members in the congregation developed visions for the new church, but I actually cautioned against this. As we neared the reality of the merger, my sermons were about being open to God's spirit, which would lead us into new truths if we were open to its leading. I preached openness and flexibility (attributes of differentiation) and asked that people not prejudge things.

Ed Friedman (1985), an early leader in applying Bowen theory to congregations, used to say that it is the job of leaders not to delegate responsibility but to delegate anxiety. I would go one step further and say, "Don't take it on at all. Leave the anxiety where it belongs." This is how I functioned in my clinical practice. The more dependent clients did everything they could to get me to take on the anxiety around their problems, to worry for them, and to come up with solutions for them. This is not helpful and it will not work. They were frustrated with me until they decided that their lives really were their responsibility. I talked with them about what they were thinking, but I did not do their thinking for them. Likewise, anxiety for the future of the church belonged to its members, not to me.

There are such things as reactive visions where a leader's vision for the church comes from personal history. While I do not remember the specifics, I know that the pastor who preceded me at this church tried to shape that church into his vision. As I listened to peoples' reports of their experiences with him, I believed that he underfunctioned in terms of his own responsibilities and overfunctioned regarding theirs. This is a guaranteed way to get oneself in unnecessary trouble (as he did) and to keep important issues in a church muddled.

My personal challenges with the merger process

The biggest personal challenge for me in this situation, in terms of differentiation, was my relationship with Bill. Even though I liked him a lot, I struggled in my relationship with him. I did not know how to label it at the time, but it would have helped if I had known something about Bowen theory then. I really had to struggle through this on my own. In terms of the theory, there were two primary issues for me in relation to Bill.

The sibling-position issue

Bill grew up with a brother and I am an only child. He got his sense of specialness, I think, through performing well and achieving in relation to his brother, and I, like most onlies, tended just to feel special whether others recognized it or not. Bill was better at working cooperatively than I was. I think Bill may have been used to being the boss in a relationship, and I was used to not having a boss. I was my own boss. I liked having his friendship, but I somewhat came to dread being a co-pastor with him. I had never had to negotiate with anyone how to fulfill my job responsibilities. Previously, I always had a lot of freedom in figuring out my job for myself within the parameters set down by the session of the church. Now I had to work with someone else who had ideas about what I should do as well as what he should do.

I think his relationship with his brother had been challenging. Like most brothers, they had their struggles and he was used to arguments and fights. I was not used to this kind of give and take. I suspect he often found me puzzling to deal with.

As an only child, I never had to compete with anyone in my family while I was growing up. I did pretty much as I wanted and did not have to share. What was mine was mine, no question about it. The idea of sharing, in general, was pretty much a foreign concept to me—until I got married. Lois is also an only child. Many of our early marital struggles simply had to do with our birth order positions. I was not good at negotiation. I identified strongly with the Lone Ranger. Those types of hero (leader) images were stuck in my head. I expected my companion to go along with what I wanted. I was bossy in my own way. One of my earliest report cards, from kindergarten, spoke of "Ronnie" being "bossy with the other children." Being an only child is not usually the best preparation for being a co-pastor.

This illustrates that the level of functional differentiation that I brought to my relationship with the congregation was different, to some extent, from what I brought to the emotionally closer relationship with Bill (or indeed, even more so in my marriage). In our closest relationships, our more basic level of differentiation emerges, and it certainly did for me with Bill.

I did not mind the challenge of hard work. I did fairly well with it, but I did not work as hard as Bill. We both liked being responsible for our own work and suddenly we had to share it. Things that might have taken either one of us fifteen minutes to decide and do on our own would often take us two hours of talking things through together. Planning a worship service together, for example, could take us hours.

From the time I was in the seventh grade right through all of my formal schooling, I worked. In all of these jobs, I found ways to both please my boss and do things the way I wanted to do them. Because we have no one to compete with, only children tend to be well tuned-in to adults as we grow up, and, not being distracted by a sibling's wishes, we can be quite good at sensing what adults (authorities) like and learning how to please them. Bill may have thought he had to compete to get praise, and I just assumed, without even thinking about it, that such praise would simply follow. Moreover, if it did not, I was not upset. I was and am my own best friend. Unlike Bill, under stress I turned inward; he quite naturally sought to talk everything out until it was absolutely clear for him. These sibling-position qualities explained a lot about our different styles of working and the challenges we both encountered with each other.

My old patterns around emotionality

I knew early on that this relationship was going to be challenging for me and it was. I think I was quite a challenge to Bill as well. The sibling differences were tough enough, but the thing that required the biggest effort at defining myself in this relationship was dealing with what I then thought of as Bill's possible anger. Whenever we encountered differences, he had an intensity about him that inspired in me a wish to back away and shut up. He never out-and-out shouted at me, but I though he could. That was my chronic anxiety at work.

My hardest work in the whole merger experience was maintaining a good working relationship with Bill, while at the same time preserving my sense of self and standing my ground whenever he became particularly intense. He was not demanding, but even so, I had difficulty dealing with our differences. It would have been possible for me to simply shut up and go along with his wishes, but I knew I would not feel good about myself and he would probably respect me less. He expected people to openly come at him with their best shot. I had to learn to be more cooperative and to share with someone who had the same responsibilities as me, and, at the same time, not to buckle under pressure just because he wanted something a particular way.

I could handle the anger of the white parents' group (see Chapter 1). It was not aimed at me personally. I had more difficulty if I was the object of the anger. Growing up with just my mother, she and I literally never had a single openly angry argument, and I never saw her argue with anyone else. I had not experienced it in a close relationship until I got married. Only then did I really begin to understand anger. Luckily, my marriage had prepared me somewhat for the relationship with Bill. In the marriage, I learned to understand and better deal with anger in a person I was close to and with my own anger. This enabled me to stay close to Bill whenever he became more intense.

If I said anything that did not add up for him, he would get that intense look (that non-verbal signal that inspired caution in me), stare at me in what I regarded as kind of challenging, and say, "What do you mean?" It was as if he thought I was hiding something from him.

I realized that I must not focus on him, or try to change him so that I could feel more comfortable, but instead to stay focused on how I wanted to be with him. If he thought that I was not being open and forthright, he would get more intense. I knew that he had felt hurt and angry in the past whenever important information in relationships had been kept from him. I learned that I had to tell him everything; I could not withhold information or keep any secrets. I told him what I had heard in my congregation, along with my own thoughts regarding the merger process. Without realizing it, with this kind of self-focus, I was enacting a key part of systems theory.

What I know now is the people whom we label paranoid have probably grown up in settings with a fair number of important secrets. Because of their sensitivity to any lack of information, some people can react with intensity, and the people close to them tend to shut up and distance, not saying anything that would further upset the other person. In effect, the distancing people are more likely to keep secrets and not say what they think in an effort to avoid dealing with what they see as the other person's intimidating anger. Their silence and distance, however, only causes the relationship to deteriorate further.

Very early in my relationship with Bill, as we entered into this merger process, I realized that I should not hold anything back. I decided I had to be entirely open and direct. Even if he did not like what I said, he could handle it better than if I did not say it. Without knowing the Bowen theory language for this, I realize now that I was staying out of triangles and that this helped the process a great deal. Because of my own uneasiness with anger, this was very difficult work for me. However, addressing this challenge, and sticking to my resolve to be open at every point, made all the difference for me in our being able to work together successfully.

Conclusion

Getting through this potentially polarizing situation for both congregations, as well as for Bill and me, took a lot of hard work, and we all did it well. Because we were involved in developing new, and somewhat unfamiliar, traditions for a new kind of church (there were no models for what we were doing as Baptists and Presbyterians), it was essential that we stick up for what we viewed as important and arrive at something that worked for all of us. These two small, humble churches managed to avoid all of the possible pitfalls and managed to make it work. I remain impressed with those people and I think that Bill and I, as leaders, did a great job as well.

7

Avoiding Polarization in a
Counseling Staff During Change

Differentiation and administration

When I was executive director of a not-for-profit counseling agency, I found Bowen theory helpful in many ways. For example, the theory helped keep me from being an overfunctioner. That way of functioning usually involves administrators in various staff alliances and intense emotional processes within both the organization and the agency's board of directors. Their anxiety often comes out of their concern for the agency or their own image as a director. I simply focused on being as much of a solid self as I could within my role and clarifying what was and was not my responsibility. Other staff members, who had responsible positions in the agency, were free to do their jobs the way they wanted. Of course, we all had well-defined contracts and guiding principles, but after that, how we did our jobs was up to each of us. I was available for consultation or conversation, but I did not control the life of the organization. I focused on what I thought was my job as executive director. Also, whenever I found myself being critical of a staff member, either aloud or silently, I presumed I was in a triangle and worked at changing myself.

Differentiation and creating change in an organization

In agencies like this, it is a common experience for one staff member to become excited about a new approach to counseling and to believe it is the answer to clients' problems, and then for that staff member to evangelize to the counseling staff for that approach. This often happens in counseling agencies, as well as in churches relating to various programmatic approaches to the life of the church. This is a source of conflict and turmoil in the agencies (and churches) because there is always a group of people who oppose any change, either because they see no value in it or because they don't want to change their practice.

This happened a great deal back in the seventies and eighties with the introduction of various family systems approaches to counseling agencies that had previously used individually-focused models like the psychodynamic model. Typically, the enthusiastic, evangelistic, family systems people would criticize the individual model that other staff members were using as inadequate. They presented their reasonable arguments about why a family systems approach was better. Often, some staff agreed with this new direction and, of course, a certain percentage of the staff resisted, and the polarizing process began around the issue of family systems approaches versus more traditional, individual models. The intensity of the polarization depended on the level of chronic anxiety in the agency rather than on the issue of which practice was better.

When I first learned about Bowen theory, I was working in the agency, but was not yet the executive director. The counselors used the more individual, psychodynamic model of counseling as their primary model of practice with their clients. In fact, my previous experience with that model was the reason I was hired by the agency. However, I somehow knew not to make a big deal out of Bowen theory once I began to learn about it, even though I was convinced that I wanted to practice it with clients. I saw its benefits for my own life, marriage, and family of origin. It worked for me, but I shut up about it with the other staff. I literally did not say a word to anyone in the agency about the theory. I only worked at trying to learn the approach as best I could by reading Bowen and learning about the practice on my own.

There was no one doing training in Bowen theory at that time on the west coast of North America. I was on my own, but I began to change my practices. At the time, the counseling staff reported on all of their new clients at weekly staff meetings. We related our take on the client's problems, gave our diagnosis, and explained how we proposed to help them. I started using family diagrams, putting my clients into the context of family, dropping the psychodynamic language and using some of the Bowen language in its place. I did not make a big deal of this or attempt to teach people anything. In fact, I did not say anything about learning a new approach. I did not offer commentary or explanations to the staff. I was doing it only for myself and had no intent of teaching anyone anything about what I was doing.

I remained respectful of other staff's ways of working and never encouraged them to think about their cases in the same way I did. In responding to other staff case presentations, I asked questions derived from my new theory. Often, the staff appreciated the fresh area of inquiry these questions opened up. Eventually, questions began to come to me from other staff members about what I was doing, and I would respond with some minimal statement that Bowen theory was no big deal, that it was just a current interest of mine and that they would not likely be interested in it. If anyone pursued me with more specific questions, I would do more of the same saying, "Oh I don't think this would be of interest to you. It's nothing special." However, in staff meetings I would continue to talk about how I was dealing with a particular case, using Bowen concepts, and what I saw happening as a result.

This was a kind of self-definition as I presented my own thinking regarding my clinical work. I was respectful to the other counselors when they told me what they thought I should think or do concerning my cases. I never argued the points. The next year, we started a post-graduate training program and I was appointed director of training. The program was for those who already had (or were working on) a degree in social work, psychology, or pastoral counseling. I organized the training using the Bowen model. The students started presenting their cases in staff meeting using Bowen theory as well. I had not let the students in on my thinking about the theory in relation to the regular staff. I kept that to myself and did not triangle with them. I did not specifically tell them how to behave with other staff, but they, perhaps taking their cue from my example, generally seemed to pick up that they were not supposed to be advocates of the approach.

Regular staff members were getting more curious about the approach, and when they asked me questions I suggested, "If you want to, you could come to a few of the training sessions and see what you think, even though it's probably not for you." Most of them took me up on this offer. They also picked up the large book of articles and other reading I provided for the training program. More and more, other staff members began to talk about their cases in terms of family systems theory. Everyone used the family diagrams. Even the executive director, Bill (not to be confused with my Baptist colleague), did so. If they misused a concept, I never corrected them or attempted to teach them anything.

From time to time in staff meetings, I talked about visiting my own family of origin and what I was doing in my own family work. This particularly aroused their interest because all of the staff had major issues with their own families. Staff in the agency began seeing the theory's personal usefulness and began picking it up for themselves at their own speed with no direct encouragement from me. We tended to hire a few of the students from our training program to be regular staff, and they added to the numbers who were working with the theory.

After several years, when I became the executive director at the agency, at the first staff meeting, I looked around at each staff member and said, "You know, it seems to me that we are primarily a Bowen family systems theory agency." Everyone nodded, "Yes." That was the first time I ever mentioned Bowen theory in a staff meeting. We may have been the very first pastoral counseling agency in North America committed to working with clients using the Bowen model. That happened without any of the typical polarizing struggles that happened in other agencies around changing their practice models.

In the church, a similar thing can happen. Someone goes to a conference (it could be on any number of topics); they become excited about something they learned, and they come back to their church preaching that approach to church life. When we do this, we say in effect, "You all should think about your church life and mission in this way." We intend this as a good thing, but it is actually the first step in starting a polarizing process. Triangles are activated around who is for and who is against the approach. Perhaps we do it because we want others to be excited and to think and believe the way we do, but that is where we fail. We feel less anxious and less alone if others agree with us. We want them to enjoy the good things from the approach that we do and share in the experience with us. Unfortunately, if there is any underlying anxiety in the church, it may begin to crystallize.

When we do this, it is possible that we are looking for validation of our beliefs. We want people on our side. Whatever the case, this is fusion-based togetherness and not intimacy or closeness. A certain number of people will agree with us and become excited about this new approach, and a certain number will not. Depending on how much anxiety is present in the church, it could become a major polarizing issue. Not all new programmatic approaches have to be handled in this way; however, anyone who pushes for a unitary way of thinking in a church is going to have this reaction; it will not result in achieving the peace and unity we strive for in the church.

Triangles, self-focus, and change

If you have something you fervently believe in, some commitment of your own, leave it at that. Let it be your "secret discipline," as Dietrich Bonhoeffer (1997) suggested. Study it and practice it in your own life as best you can, and leave the rest to God's Holy Spirit. If it is of the Truth, it will, in its own way, be persuasive. When you talk to other people about your idea and seek their support, you are likely going to mention who opposes the idea, especially if it is in any way controversial. If this is the case, you are starting a triangle and a polarizing process may result. By limiting our energy for change to our own self, acting on the principles and beliefs we have developed for our self, we act out a more-differentiated stance in our relationships. The popular phrase, "Be the change you want to see," accurately describes a self-focus stance. My behavior in my counseling center was one of self-focus rather than an other-focus.

Triangles, paradoxically, are the way we keep things the same in the church even though they are often created to bring about change. We go around looking for people who will agree with us and support us. Triangles are a way of managing our anxiety, not bringing about change. In effect, they keep an equilibrium around the status quo even though both sides may be talking about change. Triangles get in the way of relationships evolving into something new, and they remove options for new behavior in the life of the group. They lock us into a position with little flexibility.

Differentiation of self requires a self-focus rather than an other-focus or a triangular-focus. It gets us out of the self-righteous belief that we have answers for others, and it allows us to relate to others with full acceptance of who they are and how they think and whatever their position is. We do not need others to change for us to feel okay or happy. There may be appropriate times to say what we think about something, to define self openly, but if we are in any way anxiously pushy about it, or other-focused, as in "This is what you should do," it will backfire. Those times when we do speak out, it will be in the nature of, "Here I stand. This is what makes sense to me." In my early days of using Bowen theory in the staff setting, I defined myself without overtly making it a big deal. Self-definition was more often in the action rather than in the words. It was my "play on the field" with no accompanying commentary. I just did it. This way of functioning kept the anxiety lower in others because they were not being pressured to change.

Self-focus is a key aspect of differentiation. It helps us avoid triangles and simply define ourselves to others. Normally, in our more-fused way of thinking, we tend to be experts on how other people are problems in our community and what they should do to remedy the problem, but we often fail to see how we are part of the problem. An other-focus leaves us powerless and frustrated with regard to change in the community. We cannot change others. We all know this is true, but we quickly forget it when we become anxious. This will only make us more upset with others and it will lead to greater polarization.

So what do we do, for example, with the ministry of teaching in the church? Here is the key: You can only teach people when they are moving toward you, when they are motivated to learn from you. If others want to argue with you, or they are distancing from your pursuit of them, no amount of teaching will reach them. Pursuing them with your wonderful insights will only make things worse. This is what Jesus meant when he told the apostles to shake the dust from their feet whenever a village would not listen to them (*Luke* 9:5, KJV). At the agency, other staff members had to pursue me hard to get anything about the Bowen theory out of me, and even then I was stingy with it. It was really up to them to get it if they wanted it. I did not need them to imitate my practice. If no one on staff ever bought into the theory it was fine with me. I could live with that. I think it was my stance of indifference that persuaded them to learn the theory out of their own desire. They did not have to struggle with me about it, or lose self to me, or defend their own position. This left them free to think things through for themselves.

A self-focus leads to self-definition. To define self means, as I said in the fourth chapter, to think about and clarify our own goals, beliefs, values, and the principles we want to live by, and then to act on them. This focus leads us to think about how we want to live and be in relationship to others, and then to find specific ways to act on these self-defined principles. In case you have not noticed, this is a Christian way to function in life.

In the counseling agency, we gradually developed a common vision of being a pastoral counseling agency committed to Bowen theory as each person took it on. Overall, it took about four years, but it was a solid change that was made without rancor or division. The difference is that we were not attempting to define others or change them.

When one person can consistently rise out of the emotional togetherness of a system, and define a self, then others are provoked to think more clearly for themselves. Some people will not always welcome this greater differentiation of self. They may resist it initially, tell us we are wrong, and attempt to pull us back into the old togetherness. If we can hang on to our position in a non-reactive way and keep relating to them, they will eventually adapt and raise their own functional levels.

Early in the process, one staff member did keep trying to pull me back into a psychodynamic approach; I listened to him respectfully, tried to find something in what he said that I could support, and thanked him without, I hope, sounding patronizing. I encouraged him to keep working at what he was talking about and said I would look forward to hearing about his outcomes. Eventually his pursuit stopped without any sign of reactivity. He knew I had heard him and that was the critical thing for him. I reflected back to him what he was saying ("So what you are saying is. . . ?") and when he affirmed that I got his message, he was reassured. I did not argue our differing positions or try to show how he was wrong and I was right. He began to be more comfortable with our differences, and then I noticed he was slowly adopting some of my language and the concepts for himself. He, especially, caught on to the family of origin work and found the theory very useful in beginning to do his own family work. By the time I became director of the center, he was fully on board with the theory.

Clearly, this is not an approach that relies on a lot of "talking things out" and "processing" relationships. While there may be value in doing that from time to time, talking about it is useless if the polarizing process sets in. We have to relate actively to people on the other side, remaining friendly with them, asking questions that reflect our genuine interest in their thinking, while doing our own thinking about how we will act. We may try reflective listening. We can say to them, again, "So what you are telling me is . . . ? Have I got that right? Am I missing anything in what you are saying?" This lets them know we are listening, thinking about what they are saying, and getting their point. If they still try to convince us of our error, that is okay. We do not have to tell them that they are wrong or try in different ways to influence them to our thinking. We can control our own reactivity to their efforts to change us. We can stay connected to them rather than distance from them. If what they say makes sense to us, we can change our mind.

I did not want people to feel like they had to defend their intellectual territory. In this instance, if they keep pushing, then we can say, "Your approach is one way to think about things, but what continues to make sense to me is . . ." and define self's position again. I actually never had to do that with the counseling staff. We continued to act on what made sense to us, while also, figuratively, putting an arm around the person who might oppose us. This is one way to forestall the polarizing process and create change that is more effective in a system. We simply change our part in the process without pushing anyone else to do anything differently.

Conclusion

When we do not pursue people or ask them to change how they are doing things, they are more free to think for themselves. We are not instigating anxiety, reactivity, and defensiveness in them. I was able to demonstrate to the staff, through my actions, how the Bowen approach was helping me in my clinical work and in my own family life. I did not ask them to agree with me or come around to my way of thinking. I resisted any invitation they made to get me to pursue them so they could argue the points with me. This left them plenty of space to think about their own issues for themselves. They started approaching me and the Bowen theory out of their own sense of need, not out of mine.

8

A Polarized Denominational Issue Handled Well

An indirect intervention in a major denominational conflict

For seven years, I ran training programs for clergy in the application of Bowen family systems theory to ministry. Each year we accepted ten clergy into the program from a variety of denominations and theological orientations. The program ran for nine months with three-hour meetings twice a month. I ran these programs out of my pastoral counseling agency in Vancouver, British Columbia, and I ran two additional programs in other communities beyond Vancouver. For the trainees, the format focused equally on (1) learning Bowen theory, (2) examining case studies on specific acts of ministry evaluated from a Bowen theory perspective, and (3) sharing family of origin presentations.

In our training program, the examination of Bowen family systems theory with follow-up discussion was accomplished with all trainees together in a large group. The case studies and family of origin presentations were carried out in small groups. One year, the staff person who assisted me with the small groups said, "Do you know who you have in the program this year?" I said that I did not really know any of the clergy who were in the program at that time. He said, "You have a person who is the leader of those promoting the ordination of gays, and you have the leader of those opposing the ordination of gays. They are at opposite poles theologically as well." He said this with a sense of apprehension, a sense of "Now we are in for it." I said, "Great! This should be good." I knew that their denomination would be voting on the question of gay ordination in just over a year's time. I thought the timing could not be better.

These men were not friendly with each other. I remember the first day we met. One clergyman was already in the room when the other one walked in. For a moment, he appeared to consider whether he would join us; I thought he was going to turn and leave. However, he decided to come in. They acknowledged each other formally (but without any warmth), and they both took seats some distance from one another. To the surprise of my assistant, I purposely put both of them in the same small group for the year.

During the next nine months, they were both very active in the program and appeared to take to Bowen theory quite well. I had no idea what was happening in their church political life outside of the program. During the course, we never once addressed the topic of gay ordination. The focus was, quite simply, on learning Bowen theory and its application to church life. No big battles broke out between them in the group, and, in fact, they were both quite involved in each other's case study and family of origin presentations. They both did well in learning the theory and in doing their family of origin work.

At the end of the year, as part of the written evaluations, they both had very positive things to say about the program. In my follow-up phone call, I asked if there was anything else they wanted to say about the program. They agreed that the program had been extremely valuable to them, giving them strategies for more effective ministry; both said that it gave them a fresh perspective on some of the issues in their churches that concerned them. They said nothing more specific than that.

During the next six months, the denomination sponsored a series of debates about gay ordination before voting on the issue. In the end, the denomination approved ordination of gays. As one would expect, there was fallout among the more conservative churches and members of the denomination, with some members leaving it. However, I heard from several independent sources that the debates before the vote were very respectful and civil with the various advocates simply making the best case they could for their position. There was no name-calling or vilification of the other side.

A brief analysis of what happened

A year after the vote, I talked with the denominational executive about their decision to ordain gays. She told me that she was amazed at how civil the two sides were with each other. She said that was not the case in other regions across the country where there had been much more acrimony and bitterness related to the issue. In those regions, many more members had left the denomination than in her region. She did not know why things were different here. She did say the leadership on both sides was excellent and that she was proud of them. I did not tell her about their participation in my program.

I decided to call each of the men, ask how they were doing and for updates on their own family work. Then I said, "Oh, by the way . . . ," and I asked about whether they thought the program had made any difference for them regarding the gay ordination issue. They each said that, in essence, it had made a huge difference. Even though they never discussed gay ordination in our training program, they each had a much better sense of the other leader, the sincerity of his approach to ministry, and his beliefs. After listening to each other's family of origin presentations, and their involvement in the case studies, there was no way they could be negative about the intentions of the other. They said the program had taught them how emotional systems work and about effective leadership for managing those systems in their ministry. They each said that they took more responsibility for their own behavior and that, as leaders, they counseled others on their side of the issue to be as respectful as they could during the debates and during discussions with their own partisans.

I knew, in doing marital and family counseling, that people's attitudes changed when they examined their own family emotional system. They were more thoughtful and less reactive. They better understood what was happening and learned to behave differently. This developed without focusing on the primary, problematic issue that brought them in for counseling in the first place. When, at the end of counseling, I asked about that issue, they would typically say, "Oh that. We resolved that a long time ago." This proved to me that, at both family and societal levels, the immediate problem is primarily a symptom of something deeper and does not really need to be the focus of an intervention.

This is, in general, a departure from traditional mediation of disputes which involve conflict resolution practices to deal with problems. In exploring the underlying emotional system process, important issues are uncovered, which leads to new avenues for approaching the issue at hand. In fact, there is research indicating that the more people focus on an issue that divides them the more polarized and anxious they become.

Emotional cutoff and unresolved emotional attachment

Late in the development of his theory, Bowen (1978) added the concept of emotional cutoff. He described it as the "process of separation, isolation, withdrawal, running away, or denying the importance of the parental family" (382). Emotional cutoff differs from the mechanism of emotional distance discussed in Chapter 2; emotional cutoff is about distance between generations. When people cut off, they often deny the importance of the part of the family from which they distance, or that it has any continuing impact on the way they now live their adult lives. The problem is that cutoff guarantees the negative patterns of emotional process in their current relationships will be ongoing. It creates a solidification and stagnation in a person's emotional life. Those who cut off usually see the others in the family as the problem and fail to see their own participation in that family emotional process. They unconsciously replay the old family process in their adult relationships. This is when history repeats itself in their current life and relationships.

Bowen (1978) said cutoff refers to "the way people handle their unresolved emotional attachments to their parents" (382). It is reflective of their level of differentiation. Unresolved emotional attachment does not mean the "unfinished business" that therapists often refer to. It is not about unfinished arguments or particular problems or issues with particular family members that remain unchanged. It is more about the nature of peoples' emotional connection with family members and the patterns of interaction they have had. Even though people can cut off from family, they cannot cut off from the unresolved emotional attachments and the automatic, anxiety-driven emotional processes that are connected with them. Bowen's cautionary note that "time and distance do not fool an emotional system" clearly applies here. I am often reminded of the truth of this statement in my work with clients.

All of us, as a part of growing up, establish particular ways of relating to members of our family. It is a kind of pattern, or even a script. Largely, this involves the trading of and the fusion of selves in those relationships. Because it plays out so often and so intensely over the years of our development, this emotional script becomes a part of our identity. As an adult separating from our family, this emotional programming goes with us. Like method actors, we remain in character. Whatever the nature of our emotional attachments to family, positive or negative, it is a part of us.

In cutoff, we often have the illusion that the pattern is just about "them," the other family members. The thought is, "If I can get away from them, then I can be free. I can restart my life without having to deal with them and their problems. I can just be me." We tend not to understand how much of self is invested in "them." This is the part of us that is undifferentiated. In our new adult relationships, we have the same sensitivities and we function in the same ways as in our family of origin, even though the specific people involved are different. Our family themes repeat themselves in our contemporary life.

The patterns of relating and emotional functioning are present whether a person physically cuts off or not. I had a cousin, who, at the age of 46, was still living with his mother and died at that age. Like me, he was an only child and we both tended to see our nuclear family as the problem in our lives. His mother was the oldest of three children, and my mother was her younger sister. He had never left home, never married, and he was intensely involved with his family. I, on the other hand, left home with significant cutoff and rarely made contact with my mother. The illusion I had was that my mother was no longer a part of my life. Both my cousin and I had intense unresolved emotional attachment that we played out in different ways relative to our family of origin. We both distanced emotionally from family but the difference was that he stayed physically in his family.

Most of my clients worked on these themes in counseling. I will mention only one. A successful businessman came in for couple's counseling with his wife. They were having frequent arguments, some of which had to do with his business performance. She thought he could do better and be more successful. His sensitivity to her pushing him was substantial, and he had distanced from her by having an affair with a woman who was much more accepting of him (he thought). He left his wife and lived with the other woman for a year. For a time, he and the new woman contemplated marriage (after his divorce was finalized), but then he began to have the same emotional experience with this woman that he had had with his wife. Partly because of this, and because he missed his children, he dropped the other woman and reunited with his former wife.

Even so, they were still in conflict, so they came in for counseling. It turned out that he had cut off from his parents a long time ago and had not visited or talked to them for nearly fifteen years. He said that part of the issue with them was their pushing him to become a successful executive like his father. Both parents played a part in this. He found the pressure unbearable and it created huge stress for him.

Eventually, in working with him, I suggested he might go back east and visit his parents, who were now quite old, but it terrified him. He said, "No way." This man had no trouble throwing his weight around in high-powered, executive board meetings; however, he slowly became more comfortable with the idea as we talked about how he might possibly be with them without getting upset. He ended up making a number of visits, and each time he was able to do better with his level of reactivity to them when they brought up some of the same old themes. He learned to be curious about the importance of the themes in their own lives, and he began to understand that their intensity was not about him at all; it was their own unresolved emotional attachments in their families. This work had a significant impact on how he managed himself with them and in his other close relationships.

Cutoff is a matter of degrees. Some of us have significant cutoff, never seeing or having contact with one or more members of our family as adults, like this man and his parents. Some people are less cut off. We can deny the emotional impact of family on us, or we can feel so overwhelmed and dominated by it in our adult lives that we think we can never escape. Both avenues leave us with a certain degree of unresolved emotional attachment. We fail to see how the emotional patterns of our family, and our way of functioning within them, still govern our life as adults. They are a part of who we are. We have only the illusion of being grown up.

As we enter into new adult relationships, in whatever form or setting, whenever something occurs that stirs up the emotional sensitivities we developed in our families, then those old patterns and ways of functioning kick in. It is automatic. It is part of our undifferentiated self. This happens most often in marriage, but it can also happen in our relationships with our children, with those at the office, along with others in our social club or our church. The inevitable challenges and conflicts of life become the new arena in which to play out the reactive emotional scripts of the past. At least we think it is the past. In fact, that past is still very much a part of our present.

We hope that emotional cutoff will solve the emotional problems of our life, but it does not. It simply transfers the unresolved emotional attachment from the family of origin and dumps it into our new adult relationships. Bridging the cutoff, gaining knowledge about the functional facts in the emotional system of our family and our part in it, and then managing self in the midst of having close contact with members of the system can lead to differentiating a self within the system. It also lowers the level of emotional intensity and polarizing tendencies around important contemporary issues.

The two clergymen who came into the Bowen family systems training program knew they wanted to do family of origin work. Both had been cut off from parts of their families and both had unresolved emotional attachments to address. In the nine months of the program, they did some significant family work, and I know they continued the work after the training program ended. I believe this had a major impact on the manner in which they handled themselves during their denominational debates, even though neither of them had changed their beliefs about homosexuality.

Ideally, addressing the unresolved emotional attachment issues as adults (commonly referred to as doing family of origin work) is the primary way of dealing with all of this. As people reduce their level of emotional cutoff from family and then work at differentiating a self within their family, the amount of emotional intensity invested in the polarizing process is reduced, often significantly.

One main goal of the counseling I did was to initiate the work of differentiating a self within their family of origin. This meant, in part, addressing the unresolved emotional attachments with their family. As they did this, they found they had new avenues and new personal resources for addressing their contemporary relational difficulties.

Doing this work requires, first, focusing on the facts of family functioning for at least three generations. Gathering facts about the family over time is a good way to begin to connect with other family members in a new way. Then, those doing the work need to look specifically at the functioning of self within the immediate family of origin, taking note of major triangles, over- and underfunctioning behaviors, as well as other Bowen concepts. A better understanding of the sources of chronic anxiety in the family and in self is an important outcome, from which one can work more effectively at interrupting it.

At some point in this process, a person is ready to start defining self within the family and to begin acting in a more-differentiated way. This involves the kind of things I described in Chapter 4. People need to define their own beliefs and principles in terms of how they function within their families, what they will and will not do, and then act. The family often resists any change in behavior, which is the point at which the person discovers how well he or she can stick with the differentiating process. The person has to stand by self-definition, continuing to connect with family members who may be upset or angry, not entering into debates about the changed behavior, and not withdrawing from them.

It is interesting that, as the two clergymen engaged in family of origin work, each one became less reactive within the family, more objective about family functioning, and better at defining self within it, they each did a better job of dealing with controversial issues in their judicatory. It made a difference not only in their lives and their denominational functioning, but also in the way other denominational leaders functioned with them.

Conclusion

The impact of examining issues within the family of origin cannot be underestimated. Two of my books deal with how to do family of origin work. The first, *Family Ties That Bind* (1984), written for lay people, is also an introduction to family systems theory. The second, *Becoming a Healthier Pastor* (2005), specifically focuses on how the family of origin affects the work of the pastor and how, when issues with the family of origin are resolved, our relationship with the church family improves. Lay people can also make use of this book for doing their own work in family.

9

Concluding Thoughts on Leadership in Polarized Situations

Mass Appeal and the leader's differentiation of self

In 1980, Bill C. Davis wrote and produced a somewhat autobiographical play called *Mass Appeal*. It focuses on an encounter between a Roman Catholic parish priest serving a wealthy, country-club church, and a young firebrand seminarian who has radical ideas about the ordination of women and gays to the priesthood. The movie version (1984) of this play stars Jack Lemmon as the parish priest, Farley. Lemmon portrays the priest as a charming entertainer who drives a Mercedes Benz and appears to be running a social club rather than a church. He is popular and has "mass appeal" among his parishioners. The monsignor assigns Mark, the seminarian, to do an internship with Farley.

Farley and Mark instantly polarize around their approach to ministry, and they try to change each other in their hot debates. Mark says that Farley has a "song and dance theology." They argue whether it is better to "kiss ass" or "kick ass." Farley reveals his underlying cynicism about the church when he tells Mark, "If you can afford not to become a priest, tell the truth. If you want to become a priest, lie." When Mark challenges Farley's "pleasing the parishioners" style, Farley says, "I like being liked. It gives me a warm feeling and those are the only warm feelings I have." After Mark gives an angry sermon, people are upset, and Farley has to calm them down. He tells Mark,

"The pulpit is not a place to ventilate." One church member who was upset by Mark's sermon (in a classic example of unintended irony) told Farley, "I am not here to be preached to."

Farley is an excellent example of a priest fused with his congregation. Having the approval of his congregants is more important than anything. He lives for their praise and they love to be emotionally massaged by him. He is also a depressed secret drinker who spends his evenings with a bottle, and he has no friends. He was emotionally and physically abused by his father while growing up and has been looking for someone to approve of him ever since. Mark is fused with the Church, which is manifested by his rebellion against it. He is also clearly fighting emotional battles with his wealthy, influential father and his family. Both Farley and Mark are emotionally cut off from their families and have significant unresolved emotional attachments.

As they continue their debates, they gradually get to know one another and learn about the other's struggles in life. Each one's connection to the other increases as they become more open and vulnerable with one another. Both are hesitant to move closer and accept the other's friendship. Mark begins to open up about his own struggles with his sexuality. Farley struggles with whether or not to support Mark in becoming a priest. At one point Farley says, with regard to the congregation, "Maybe we've got this problem in reverse. It is not so much to get the people to like you as for you to like the people." He asks Mark, "What do you feel for these people?" and Mark says that he loves them. Farley challenges him, saying, "How? You show your love by offending them?"

Mark accuses Farley of being a phony and not caring for his congregants. In anger, he says, "They are pouring their guts out to a drunk who pretends to be a priest." Farley admits that it is he who needs them. Mark responds, "What you believe has to be more important than what your congregation thinks of you."

Farley's painful answer is, "I don't know what I believe anymore."

Even though he continues to struggle with Mark, Farley begins to support Mark's ordination in spite of the monsignor's opposition. At the end, Mark is ready to leave the church, but he stays to hear one more of Farley's sermons. In it, a sober Farley says to the congregation, "I can't do this anymore. I never cared enough to run the risk of losing you . . . . My need for your love has kept me silent." He then asks the congregation to support Mark in his struggle with the monsignor to become a priest. At the end of the sermon, Mark walks out of the church, passing the sign with that morning's sermon topic, "On the Road to the Priesthood."

I found this story to be a powerful tale of what many pastors and lay people struggle with; that is, "How much do I dare to let people know who I am and what I believe?" It also raises questions of how a pastor or leader cares for the people in the church and what is the most caring way to behave. Apart from a focus on the contentious issues of ordination, and what should or should not happen, for me, the most important issues in this play relate to cutoff from family, the unresolved emotional attachments, and how these issues affect the church leader's ministry. Addressing these issues will help us to become better church leaders. In the movie, as Mark and Farley begin to address these concerns, I think they will change and finally become better priests.

The "I" position, emotional connection, and change

Offering his thinking about how change happens in a family, Bowen (1978) asserted:

> When one member of a family can calmly state his own convictions and beliefs, and take action on his convictions without criticism of the beliefs of others

and without becoming involved in emotional debate, then other family members will start the same process of becoming more sure of self and more accepting of others (252).

Bowen is describing change in systems through the "I" position. This happens when someone in an emotional system takes a self-focused approach to difficult situations (in contrast to an other-focus). I saw change happen repeatedly in counseling when one person in a family, or a couple, could achieve the six goals implied in his assertion:

- achieve an inner calmness (lowered level of anxiety);
- think through self's own principles, beliefs, and convictions;
- state his or her own convictions and beliefs;
- take action on them;
- refuse to criticize the beliefs of others; and
- refuse to become involved in emotional debate with others in the system who react to the person's self-focused action.

When one person can take this more thoughtful stance, in other words, differentiate a self, while continuing to relate closely to other people in the system, eventually others will become more thoughtful about their own position and become, in Bowen's words, "more accepting of others."

Even though Bowen is talking about family therapy, his point equally applies to any group of closely related people, for example, a congregation and its leaders. Elsewhere he said, "The successful introduction of a significant other person into an anxious or disturbed relationship system has the capacity to modify relationships within the system" (342). Within a congregation, we do not usually have to focus on introducing a "significant other" (remember, he was talking about the introduction of a therapist into a relationship). However, it does apply to my "introduction" into the white parents' group. That was a success.

Quite often, church leadership serves for several years. However, such long-standing leaders had to develop some significance to or for the congregation to be successful over a number of years. A new pastor, though, does not always achieve that connection quickly. He or she eventually has to count for something with the congregation emotionally. This means that people begin to see the leader as invested in their future as a church and of some kind of value to them personally. This usually takes time.

The leader has to develop a viable relationship with the members and be able to maintain that relationship during difficult and stressful times. If the leader distances, or becomes involved in a triangle, of any sort, then things will not improve. Finally, this strategy does not promise that all problems will be solved and any crisis averted or resolved. It simply provides a method for modifying the emotional process in the church so there is a better chance of improving the situation. At a minimum, tension will be reduced and people can think more clearly. This essentially describes how I was present with the white parents' group (Chapters 1-2), and how Edna was present with others in the church merger (Chapter 6).

In the case of two people, or factions, in a church who are in polarized positions, a third, neutral (non-triangled) person is necessary as a resource for them. Each of the opposing parties look for the support of leadership in the church and try to pull leaders into the triangle. An effective leader resists participating in a triangle, but at the same time maintains an appropriate emotional connection to both sides. Change depends on the leader's ability to do this and to be interested in the experiences of all of those involved in the polarizing situation.

Obviously, leaders need a clear understanding of triangles (and self's own vulnerability to them) in order to know how to relate to both sides and to be neutral around their debate, not taking a side. This understanding will probably be most successful if the leader has examined his or her history with triangles in his or her own family. It is through that examination that a leader will learn best about self's own vulnerabilities to triangles. The leader needs to be comfortable with whatever accusations may come. For example, some will say things like, "If you don't agree with us, you are not a Christian." In spite of that, the leader must not distance from or react with counterattacks on the accusers. While group members might be upset with the leaders for not declaring what side they are on, in the long run, people greatly appreciate this stance.

With the white parents' group, it would not have worked for me to state openly everything I thought with regard to their situation or my personal stance on racism. I was not dishonest with them, but I was not fully open. I remained as neutral as I could. I was not sufficiently connected to them to make open "I" position statements. They would have rejected me. My "I" position was evident in how I was present with them and how I related to them, rather than through openly stating my beliefs, and that is what worked. If the sense of connection is not there, there can be no meaningful act of differentiation. Whatever the leader does, without that connection, has no impact. At best, such unsuccessful efforts are considered irrelevant, and, at worst, hostile.

When a leader has a suitable connection with the group, following Bowen's advice is much easier. This would be true of a pastor or a lay leader who has become important to the congregation. Edna, whom I described in Chapter 6, was this kind of leader; she had a strong connection with the church community, and she never openly promoted a specific agenda. During the church merger process, her strength of character and her straightforward manner helped me deal with the congregation as they thought through this issue. Father Farley finally gave a good, self-defining sermon at the end of the movie. He made a strong statement about supporting Mark for ordination, but what counted most was that, now, he could maintain his position when opposition arises, which it will. Bowen makes clear that it is essential to act on what we say.

What is a good emotional connection?

Farley was able to speak to his people in a straightforward way because of the nature of his relationship with them. Most of the congregation's members liked him. His connection with them was not what it could be, but it was good enough. In order to lead as a solid, well-differentiated self, leaders need to be well connected to those they wish to lead. The connection has to be real—and recognized. Just being an officeholder or being identified by a title does not automatically give us a recognizable connection. Leaders have to be emotionally important to those they wish to lead. This is necessarily a given within a family, regardless of the emotional valence—positive or negative—of the connection.

Leaders, as well as their followers, have to understand that "Who you are, what you think, and how you act count for something to me." Leaders have to have a sense of respect and appreciation for the other church members. Prior to the act of differentiation, leaders have to be known for acting on the behalf of the group, of caring for the well-being of the group. They need to be seen as representing what is good for the group without taking responsibility for the group or by overfunctioning.

Overfunctioners are often well-liked leaders (a frequent congregational phenomenon), but it is uncertain that they really hold the group in high esteem, that they really care for the group, even though all of their actions appear to be on behalf of the group, even to the point of self-sacrifice. Their need for the group to be less adequate and more dependent on them influences their leadership and makes them feel good about self. Like Farley, that is how they get feelings of being liked. This is fusion. Differentiated leaders know what they are and are not responsible for, and they respect the group enough to know that others have to think through their own positions and take responsibility for their own actions. That was my intent with the church merger I described in Chapter 6.

As with Paul's organic image of the body in *First Corinthians*, all parts need to have an appreciation of what the other parts do and how they function to maintain the body's health and well-being. If the leader does not regard some parts of the body as important, or does not think that they count or have standing, then that segment of the church community reacts negatively to the actions of the leader.

Differentiation of self and action

Differentiation is primarily about action, not words. What we say and what we do can be quite different. People believe our actions more than our words. Words serve to interpret our actions, and they are empty if they have no connection to our actual behavior. Too many people think that differentiation is about saying something that others may find provocative. This is the way many leaders unnecessarily get themselves in trouble.

With regard to the change in my counseling agency (Chapter 7), I also acted with minimal words. The words came much later after the staff had moved voluntarily toward the Bowen system. With regard to the two clergy on opposite sides of the gay ordination question (Chapter 8), it was the act of putting them together in the same small group that made the difference. I did not say a word to anyone about doing this, not even to my staff colleague who was concerned about what might happen between the two men. It was the same with the two congregations coming together to form a union church (Chapter 6). There were very few words on my part.

Emotional connection, as with differentiation, is more about action than words. With the white parents' group, my actions were the most important ingredient. I kept words to a minimum. I was defining myself to them in how I related to them. With my colleagues and friends back then, I used more words to justify what I was doing, and my words did not help all that much. They had difficulty with my actions and defined them as negative. If I had merely talked about what we should do, without acting on my beliefs with the parents' group, it would have been an interesting debate and my colleagues would not have been as offended. But then again, without action, I would not have been successful with the parents' group; my actions with the group not only defined me, but built the emotional connection I needed to guide them effectively.

People are highly reactive to words and ideas. This is the arena of many polarized debates. However, they have to struggle more with interpreting actions that are not immediately clear and obvious in their meaning. They have to think differently. When the president of the white parents' group demanded to know why I was working with the group, he was commenting on two different types of church action toward him and the people he represented. He was puzzled that I was not behaving like previous church leaders had behaved. Like his Catholic priests, I could have said provocative, other-focused words about their racism, and they would have distanced from me. We would not have connected. My action said something different, and it gradually made me more important to them. My only words of self-definition were to the effect of, "It seems to me that what we are dealing with is important and attention needs to be paid." I did not use racist language in talking with them and in leading group discussion, nor did I react to their invective; even so, I believe they understood that I did not share their racist feelings.

The active ministry of listening

Carl Rogers (1951), the 1950s psychotherapist and former seminary student, called his primary clinical technique, "active listening." The therapist echoes the client's words as a means of demonstrating that he is listening closely. For example, when I said things like, "So what you are saying is . . . ?", I was using this technique.

This is a good practice and it describes an important ministry. Listening is a good way of defining self to others. We cannot debate people who are heavily invested in a polarized position. I mean, we can, but it will not go anywhere, and we may become one of them, or, rather, one of the people on the other side. We will be in the triangle and unable to minister to them. A good friend of mine, Doug Anderson, reminded me of a quote by the lay theologian and lawyer William Stringfellow (1967). "Listening is a rare happening among human beings. Listening is a primitive act of love in which one person makes himself accessible and vulnerable to another person's word."

I have been on the receiving end of this kind of love. When I was at Princeton Seminary back in the early 1960s, I was a young, polarizing evangelical in what I then regarded as a liberal seminary. I was headed for a ministry in one of the large west coast, evangelical churches. I had a reputation for arguing with my professors because of their liberal theology, and I was considered an articulate representative of my position. To help pay for my education, I also worked in the seminary dining hall with an older man named George Morey (his real name). He is long dead now. He was headwaiter and I was assistant headwaiter. George had left a life in business in his fifties to become a pastor. We spent a lot of time together. George liked me, and he was friendly toward me. However, I felt the need to debate him, to convince him of "my truth," and bear witness to him. While I also liked him, I regarded him as a heathen and questioned how he could have any ministry at all with his very liberal ideas and "bad" theology.

Unlike some of the other, more liberal students who did not agree with me and kept their distance, George stayed connected with and interested in me. He listened to me, and he asked me questions rather than debating me. Occasionally he would say what he believed about his own call to ministry and what made it important to him. He was never offensive toward me even though I know he disagreed sharply with me. I am sure I was offensive toward him but he never reacted. George did not try to change my beliefs, but his questions were searching, and they made me think about what I was saying. I liked it, but I did not let him know. My responses were intentionally argumentative.

George was warm and friendly toward me, and he stayed interested in me in spite of my often offensive remarks to him about his faith, or rather, what I thought was his lack of it. He was not put off or threatened by my ideas and attitude. He moved toward me with interest rather than distancing from me with disdain and disagreement. Although many other factors were involved, I consider George to be one of the main reasons I went into urban ministry. It was there, through his ministry, that George's questions began to ring clearly in my ears, as I encountered the real life of people in the inner city. I began to see what he was talking about with regard to ministry. I also began to realize that George was the best pastor I had ever had.

George was a powerful example of someone who had accomplished the six goals I extracted from a Bowen quotation earlier in this chapter. That is, he had achieved a remarkable inner calmness; it was evident that he had always thought through his principles, beliefs, and convictions; he clearly stated his convictions and beliefs, no matter how strongly I argued with him; he was a man who acted upon his convictions and beliefs; he steadfastly refused to criticize my beliefs; and he refused to engage in an emotional debate with me even when I was critical of him.

In addition, he listened and he asked questions. That was his primary ministry to me. George tried to evoke my best thinking around many topics. He was not trying to debate me or convince me of the truth of his positions. I am sure he regarded much of what I said as, at best, naive, and I was. However, he did not criticize or ridicule me. Asking questions that evoke peoples' best thinking is an excellent form of ministry. Much of my work in counseling has become just this kind of activity.

Questions are tricky things. We often disguise statements in our questions. In our ministry to polarized people, we must not ask questions with the intent of changing their minds or getting them to agree with us. If that is the case, they will react and hear our questions as statements and as challenges. If our questions have the slightest hint of, "Do you really think . . . ," or "Don't you think . . . ," the other person will hear our agenda and back away. At their best, questions are not a way of arguing with others. If they do not come out of a genuine interest in the way the other person makes sense of life, then they are useless.

Defining self with our questions

Asking questions is a way of defining self without being argumentative in polarized circumstances. If the questions do not have a hidden agenda for challenging or changing the other person, and if they reveal only a neutral stance within the emotional system, they represent a positive way of positioning self within an emotional system. The ability to ask nonconfrontational and thought-provoking questions is a matter of differentiation of self. We do not have an agenda for others, and we respect their thinking while engaging them with interest. Questions define self because they reveal an active way of relating to another that is clear about the space between self and other, without anxiety on our part. A question implies a position. In this case, the position is a nonthreatening interest in the other's way of making sense of the world.

Questions help to bring in new information, to provoke thinking, to broaden the understanding of problems, and to broaden the perspective. By making things more complex, less simple, bringing in more factors to consider, we can open up new avenues of approach. People tend to want a black-and-white, simple, right or wrong world, especially around polarized issues. This is rarely possible, however, in reality. By enlarging the context, bringing in more elements and facets, we can better understand what looks to us like crazy and irrational behavior, such as the anger of the white parents.

People in the church frequently approach controversial issues by keeping silent, avoiding discussion of anything that would possibly be contentious. Being silent around controversial issues is not an alternative to debating them. Being silent about these issues does not change things. We can thoughtfully engage others and not ignore the important issues of life as well as uphold the idea of diversity in community. My friend George Morey proved this to me, and he helped to broaden my world and my thinking—although it took time for me to realize it. This sort of response holds the other in esteem in spite of their disagreement. If we ignore, or are uninterested, or have contempt, we cannot be pastoral. If the other's words trigger our own reactivity, then we are no longer demonstrating that we care about them.

Questions and the life force for individuality

One thing I look for in response to my questioning is any sign of the person's independence from the group they represent. I want to support their self-definition, to encourage them to think less about party line or group rhetoric and more about trying to figure things out for self. The direction is for them to think things through for themselves rather than just repeat some political mantra. The goal is not to convert people to our own way of thinking. It is simply to stimulate thoughtfulness. The only way people begin to think for themselves is through direct experience with someone who is not threatening, who does not seek or demand conformity, who listens without challenging or stimulating opposition. My experience is that people appreciate this regardless of whether they say it or not.

In addition to a life force for togetherness, we all have a life force for individuality. It is about being our own person. Polarized people are usually fused into the group that provides them the rhetoric to explain the nature of their anxiety. While it feels good to be in a group (togetherness) and to be supported by them, the nature of this fusion is to override individuality. In spite of this, people want to be seen as individuals, as thinking people in their own right. They like to have their own individuality evoked and recognized. We can ask about them personally whenever possible, rather than debate their beliefs or positions as such.

Asking questions about what people believe can be tricky. The problem with asking content-oriented questions is that we will be tempted, at some point, to debate their responses. This is fusion which, for us, is uncomfortable given the differences of others. Their responses tend to come from the rhetoric of their group. We get group-think from them rather than their own personal thinking. We must avoid debating these content-based, group-think responses. If peoples' minds could be changed by simple argumentation then it would have happened long ago. Polarized positions are rarely resolved through reason; they are emotional positions, and reason, however faulty, is used to defend these positions. Emotionality has reason of its own, and a direct reasonable response is not the antidote.

Thoughtful questions that do not directly challenge the person's thinking, but only hope to enlarge it and identify unnoticed holes in the thinking, can be an effective way to relate. What are they not considering in taking their stance? Can they look ahead to see what what will happen if their approach is adopted? The point of the questioning is to stimulate and to enhance individual thinking, to short circuit the automatic "we" thinking, to evoke more individuality out of the fused togetherness with their group, and to get evaluation that is more critical from the person.

The individuality force in a person may be weak at first. The leader can encourage this individuality by taking a new approach to asking questions—encouraging them to think about self and self's part in it all, and what self will or will not do. Even so, the leader must avoid taking a side, while, at the same time, supporting the emerging individuality. The togetherness side will often present as the more righteous, or virtuous, or loving side, and this is tricky for the leader. We do not want to debate or argue their reactivity and emotional arguments, but instead, to go with them to the anxiety behind their reactive process without making it obvious. One type of question I ask frequently, after someone speaks about self is, "I find what you just said about yourself very interesting. How did you figure that out for yourself?"

With regard to their conflict, we can explore specifics relating to the other side. Without actually labeling it, it helps if people can become aware of the automatic, reactive process that goes on between them and others. Are they happy with this way of relating? How would they like to do it? Had they ever thought of any other way to do it, or how to interrupt it? The intent here is to stimulate thinking about self's part in the conflict, and what its value is. How did they arrive at their own position? What do they bring to it from their own background? How did this conflict begin to develop? What tipped them over the edge so that the hostility level went up? What was this about and does it relate to anything in their own backgrounds?

When my clients talk about self, it grabs my interest and I pursue the issue of individuality and self-definition. My questions are designed to find the "I" within the "We." I may ask a number of questions: What is the history of a person's thinking? What makes the position especially important? How did it come about? How does it affect self in relation to others? What is the person's goal? How will things change if that goal is achieved? Are they in total agreement with every point that their leaders say? On what points do they differ? Every response about self should evoke more questions from us that invite the person to go further. When they stop talking, and begin to distance, we respect that and do not pursue. If we pursue, we are caught up in an emotional process.

I do not focus specifically on, "What do you feel?" Feelings will come up and it is fine to talk about them. I would not encourage the direct expression of them, but describing them is fine. I never try to get people to alter their feelings. The fact is their feelings will change when they have been able to change their position in the larger emotional system, or in relation to their opponents. Feelings are connected to our position in the emotional system. A changed position leads to changed feelings.

Bowen (1978) said, "The togetherness force defines [people] as being alike in terms of their beliefs, philosophies, life principles and feelings" (218). Under the influence of togetherness, they use the pronoun "we" a great deal. Self gets lost in this language. Jesus, when speaking with various people in the gospels, rarely treated them as part of a group. He usually spoke with them and treated them as individuals, capable of doing their own thinking. Those who opposed him came at him with their group-think positions. He sought to get them to think about their beliefs, as with the lawyer and the parable of the Good Samaritan. In essence, his questions asked, "Okay, this is the party line about Samaritans, but what do you think?" His model is one that pastoral counselors can follow. If the clients are comfortable with the questioner and do not think there is any kind of agenda behind the questions, they will find such questions useful.

My belief is that many polarized people are not very comfortable with either their position or their behavior. I think that a part of them struggles with the positions they have taken. I take the vehemence of their positions as evidence of this. They know they are very reactive and that it is not constructive. I think a part of them (usually unrecognized) would like to get along better with others and be able to discuss important issues in ways that are more positive. I think most of the white parents knew others saw them as racists, and they did not really like being seen that way, but their anxiety-driven reactivity took over their lives. Whenever one of them said to me, "Excuse me Father, but I have to say this . . . ," they were acknowledging this fact. As they became less anxious and clearer about their goals—which were not racist goals—I think they were happy to show a different side of themselves in the mixed-race groups. Those groups gave them a chance to feel better about themselves. Early on, no one could have imposed these groups on them saying, "This is what you should do." The groups were part of a natural development that came out of their own work and thinking things through for themselves.

Change happens when people discover something that helps them with their own self-defined problems. Friendly questions help them discover and open new avenues to explore. Bowen theory gives people a new way of looking at their lives and it happens entirely on their own terms. It is not imposed from without. In doing counseling, as people begin to listen better to my questions and think for themselves, I gradually begin to tell them my own beliefs about emotional process and the nature of their relational difficulties. If they show interest, I continue. If they react or do not connect, I back off and ask more questions. Asking questions helps people to sort these things through for themselves. Our questions can be a primary resource for them to better define themselves.

In addition to the statements that people make about self, our questions need to evoke thinking about the functional facts of a situation: who does what, when, and how? A focus on facts, rather than opinions and beliefs, will be more concrete. Of course, facts are often debatable in polarized situations, and one set of facts may be given more importance than others. Often there is lack of agreement about what is factual. Nevertheless, we should not debate the facts. The larger issue is the level of emotionality that people bring to the issues that will often decide what is accepted as factual. As I have said, this is essentially about unresolved emotional attachment in the family of origin. It never works to interpret this for people, telling them this or that is what is really going on. It has to be a discovery of their own.

Therefore, in addition to questions around any hotly debated issues, and the way self ("I") is invested in them, we can be interested in people's family life and experience. "How does this issue play out within your family?" However, asking these kinds of questions is also tricky, and going slowly may be required. People can be highly reactive to our interest in their family, and hesitant to be open about their experience in their family. Questions in this realm require a higher level of trust and confidence that the questioner has no special agenda. When people feel safe, they appreciate being able to talk about self in family. It is one of the most important aspects of their lives and they rarely find someone who is interested without needing to tell them what to do about it.

Once the safety threshold is crossed, they will begin to be more open and thoughtful. For that reason, an essential question for a leader is, "How can I be a safe presence for others?" Being less anxious is the basic first step. Not triangling, in spite of their invitations to do so, is next. Moving toward the person with interest in who they are without a change agenda follows, and, finally, not pursuing them when they distance. Let them be in charge of the degree of closeness in your relationship. Often a mutual interest in some other field that is noncontroversial is a good way to connect and to develop a level of safety.

Conclusion

In the preface, I told the story of the Good Samaritan. The lawyer came to Jesus and asked him a question that came out of his own intensely polarized tribal debates. He invited Jesus into the triangle by asking his position on, "Who is my neighbor?" Instead of answering the question, Jesus told him the story of the Good Samaritan, which reframed the issue. Then Jesus asked him a question about how he defined himself. Rather than the question, "Who is my neighbor?" which could lead to endless debates about who was acceptable and who was not, or who was too different and, therefore, could not be a neighbor, Jesus asked, in essence, "Are you being a neighbor?" The lawyer's question came from his tribal rhetoric and argumentation. Jesus asked a self-focused question, designed to evoke thinking about self.

Polarization requires two sides that are willing to line up in opposition to each other and fight it out. If just one side continues to relate to the other, not going into opposition mode, then things can change—eventually. It is that word, "eventually," that instigates our struggle with what I have been saying here. Our impatience is a sign of our own fusion, and our continued participation in the polarizing process. On the other hand, it isn't patience that we need because patience means waiting for someone else to act—waiting for them to change. If this is the case, then we are not out of the polarizing stance no matter how clever we are. If we are being patient with others, we could be in a triangle. We are neither neutral nor differentiated.

It takes a strong sense of self, a higher level of differentiation, to connect to others with whom we deeply disagree and resist an investment in changing them. This means that the primary challenge we face is the one Jesus proposed. How do we define ourselves? Are we a neighbor to those who differ from us? In order to be the self we want to be, do we have to have others agree with us and support us? Or can we be with them, be interested in their welfare, and not have to have them be different?

I think it is worth repeating the words of Michael Kerr (1988):

> The higher the level of differentiation of people in a family or a social group, the more they can cooperate, look out for one another's welfare, and stay in adequate contact during stressful as well as calm periods. The lower the level of differentiation, the more likely the family [or social group like the church], when stressed, will regress to selfish, aggressive, and avoidance behaviors; cohesiveness, altruism, and cooperativeness will break down (93).

This clearly describes what happens in churches that have been affected by the polarizing process. It also points us in the direction we need to move when trying to overcome this process. The higher the level of differentiation we have, the better we can be a neighbor to those who differ from us.

Selected Bibliography

Bonhoeffer, Deitrich. *Letters and Papers from Prison*, New York: Touchstone, 1997.

Bowen, Murray. *Family Therapy in Clinical Practice*. New York: Jason Aronson, 1978.

Comella, Patricia, "Emotional Process in Society: the 8th Concept of Bowen Theory," *Choptank Perspectives* (blog), http://choptankperspectives.wordpress.com/2011/12/22/chapter-1-emotional-process-in-society-the-8th-concept-of-bowen-theory, December 22, 2011

Davis, Bill C. *Mass Appeal*. New York: Dramatists Play Service, Inc.,1982.

Friedman, Edwin H. *Generation to Generation: Family Process in Church and Synagogue*. New York: Guildford, 1985.

Kerr, Michael E., and Bowen, Murray. *Family Evaluation: The Role of Family as an Emotional Unit That Governs Individual Behavior and Development*. New York: Norton, 1988.

Mass Appeal, directed by Glenn Jordan. 1984; (Universal City, CA: Universal Studios,1992), DVD.

Papero, Daniel V. *Bowen Family Systems Theory*. Boston: Allyn and Bacon, 1990.

Richardson, Lois, and Richardson, Ronald W. *Birth Order and You: How Your Sex and Position in the Family Affects Your Personality and Relationships*. Vancouver: Self-Counsel, 1990.

Richardson, Ronald W. *Becoming a Healthier Pastor: Family Systems Theory and the Pastor's Own Family. Creative Pastoral Care and Counseling.* Minneapolis: Fortress Press, 2005.

———. *Becoming Your Best: A Self-Help Guide for Thinking People.* Minneapolis: Augsburg Books, 2008.

———. *Couples in Conflict: A Family Systems Approach to Marriage Counseling.* Minneapolis: Augsburg Books, 2010.

———. *Creating a Healthier Church: Family Systems Theory, Leadership, and Congregational Life.* Creative Pastoral Care and Counseling. Minneapolis: Fortress Press, 1996.

———. *Family Ties That Bind: A Self-Help Guide to Change through Family of Origin Therapy.* Vancouver: Self-Counsel Press, 1984.

Rogers, C. R. *Client-centered Therapy.* Boston: Houghton Mifflin, 1951.

Stringfellow, William. *Count It All Joy.* Grand Rapids, MI: Eerdmans Publishing Company, 1967.

Titelman, Peter. *Clinical Applications of Bowen Family Systems Theory.* New York: Haworth Press, 1998.

Toman, Walter. *Family Constellation: Its Effects on Personality and Social Behavior,* 4th Edition. New York: Springer Publishing Company, 1993.

Bowen Family Systems Theory Training Opportunities

Bowen Center for the Study of the Family
4400 MacArthur Boulevard NW, Suite 103
Washington, D.C. 20007
Phone: (800) 432-6882 or (202) 965-4400
www.thebowencenter.org
Email: info@thebowencenter.org

Bowen Family Systems Clinical Seminars
7301 Mission Road
Prairie Village, Kansas
phone: (913) 722-1010
www.bfsclinicalseminars.com

Center for Family Consultation
820 Davis Street, Suite 504
Evanston, Illinois 60201
www.thecenterforfamilyconsultation.com
email: info@thecenterforfamilyconsultation.com

Center for Family Process
10601 Willowbrook Dr.
Potomac, MD 20854
Phone: (301) 340-3152
www.centerforfamilyprocess.com

Center for the Study of Human Systems
313 Park Ave. #308, Falls Church, VA 22046
Phone: (703) 532-1501
www.hsystems.org

Center for the Study of Natural Systems and the Family
PO Box 701187
Houston, Texas 77270-1187
Phone (713) 790-0226
www.csnsf.org

CSNSF Border Programs
El Paso, Texas
Phone: (443) 623-4021
www.csnsf.org/borderprograms

Clergy Seminars in Family Process
205 W. Obell St.
Whitehall, Michigan 49461
Phone: (231) 893-8525
www.clergyseminars.net

Florida Family Research Network
2173 NW 99th Ave.
Doral, Florida 33172
Phone: (561) 279-0861
email: ebgfamilycenter@comcast.net

Healthy Congregations
2199 E. Main Street
Columbus, Ohio 43209
Phone: (614) 384-4611
www.healthycongregations.com

KC Center for Family and Organizational Systems
3100 NE 83rd Street, Suite 2350
Kansas City, Missouri 64119
Phone: (816) 436-1180, ext. 4
www.kcfamilysystems.com
email: info@kcfamilysystems.org

The Leader's Edge
10601 Willowbrook Drive
Potomac, Maryland 20854
Phone: (301) 299-7475
www.coachingleadership.com
email: crimone@coachingleadership.com

Leadership in Ministry
9506 Heather Spring Drive
Richmond, Virginia 23238
Phone: (804) 965-0647
www.leadershipinministry.org
leadershipinministry@gmail.com

The Learning Space
4545 42nd St. NW, Suite 201
Washington, D.C. 20016
Phone: (202) 966-1145
www.thelearningspacedc.com

Living Systems
209-1500 Marine Drive
North Vancouver, BC Canada bv7p 1t7
Phone (604) 926-5496
www.livingsystems.ca
email: livingsystems@telus.net

New England Seminar on Bowen Theory
25 A Medway Street
Dorchester, Massachusetts 02124
www.bowentheoryne.org
email: contact@bowentheoryNE.org

The Prairie Center for Family Studies
Manhattan, Kansas
www.theprairiecenter.com

Princeton Family Center for Education, Inc.
PO Box 331
Pennington, New Jersey 08534
Phone: (609) 924-0514
www.princetonfamilycenter.org

Programs in Bowen Theory
Sebastopol, California
www.programsinbowentheory.org
email: info@programsinbowentheory.org

Southern California Training in Bowen Theory and Psychotherapy
625 Third Avenue
Chula Vista, California 91910
Phone: (619) 525-7747
www.socalbowentheory.com
email: info@socalbowentheory.com

Vermont Center for Family Studies
PO Box 5124
Essex Junction, Vermont 05453-5124
Phone: (802) 658-4800
email: thompsonleadership@gmavt.net

Western Pennsylvania Family Center
733 North Highland Ave. Pittsburgh, PA 15206
Phone: (412) 362-2295
Pittsburgh, PA
www.wpfc.net and info@wpfc.net

Working Systems
4545 42nd Street NW, Suite 201
Washington, D.C. 20016
Phone: (202) 966-2265
www.workingsystemsinc.net

Workplace Solutions
168 Battery Street
Burlington, Vermont 05401
Phone: (800) 639-1596
www.workplacesolutionsvt.com

More Information on Dr. Murray Bowen and His Work

To learn more about Dr. Murray Bowen and Bowen family systems theory visit http://ideastoaction. wordpress.com/audio-files-and-video-files. Here you will learn about *Leaders for Tomorrow*, a 401(c)(3) organization, which was established to assist the National Library of Medicine's effort to preserve the original papers and videos of Dr. Murray Bowen and make his comprehensive and impressive archives accessible to the public.

Soon, *Leaders for Tomorrow: The Murray Bowen Archives Project*, will launch a website dedicated to preserving Dr. Bowen's work, along with ongoing papers, books and records of meetings and conferences that enhance his legacy and the work he began.

CPSIA information can be obtained at www.ICGtesting.com
Printed in the USA
LVOW092001150612

286349LV00020B/150/P